HIGH ON LIFE

HIGH ON LIFE

How to Naturally Harness
the Power of Six Key Hormones
and Revolutionize Yourself

DAVID J. P. PHILLIPS

PEGASUS BOOKS
NEW YORK LONDON

HIGH ON LIFE

Pegasus Books, Ltd.
148 West 37th Street, 13th Floor
New York, NY 10018

Copyright © 2024 by David J. P. Phillips

First Pegasus Books cloth edition May 2024

ISBN: 978-1-63936-698-9

10 9 8 7 6 5 4 3 2 1

Printed in the United States of America
Distributed by Simon & Schuster
www.pegasusbooks.com

Contents

Introduction

Sometimes you ask for things and then receive them – only not in the way you expected!

It all changed for me on a murky autumn day in November. My wife Maria and I had gone out for a walk, when out of nowhere, as we were crossing a bridge, I was struck by a sensation I had never experienced before in my adult life. I paused, frozen by the shock of it. Maria looked at me, tilted her head to one side, as she often does, and asked me, 'What's the matter, love?' I tried my best to describe to her how I felt. She gave off a little surprised laugh, and told me, 'That sounds like happiness to me.' Five minutes later, the feeling had passed and the dark emptiness I was used to had returned. However, our story actually begins before that day.

A few months earlier, I had been in Gothenburg on a lecturing trip. I was giving a keynote speech on communication, which only makes what I'm about to relate to you all the more embarrassing. After finishing the first half of my lecture, I declared that it was time for a break. I remained at my computer, doing nothing in particular. This is a gambit we lecturers sometimes use at half-time, in the hope that somebody will walk up to us to give us a pat on the shoulder and a compliment. It's a nice way to get energized for the second half. And indeed, in the corner of my eye, I spotted a woman approaching. Her hesitant gait, and the way she cautiously leaned into my private space, however, made it plain that what I was about to receive was definitely not a compliment. Instead, she told me, 'I just thought you should know that you've been consistently using our competitor's name instead of ours in all your examples.' I thought I was going to sink through the floor . . . *How could this be happening? I'm a rhetorician. I weigh every last word with great care before uttering it.* But this wasn't the first time this had happened.

On the train, heading home, I thought to myself, *My career is over! If I don't even know what I'm saying, how can I say anything at all?* The event in Gothenburg was the straw that broke the camel's back, and I made an appointment to see my family doctor. Again.

'David, *what did I tell you last time?*' His words were heavy with reproach. 'You came here two years ago, complaining about twitches in your face. I told you that they were caused by stress, and that you needed to slow down, do less and recover. Then you came back last year, complaining about stomach and heart issues. I told you the same thing then, and now you're back, *again,* telling me that your *stress* is causing you neurological problems! How am I ever going to get through to you? If you don't change your life now, you could end up with incurable problems. In my estimation, you'll need at least three years to go back to where you were – and there's no way to speed that up, so don't even think of trying!'

I left with my tail between my legs and tears streaking down my face, and proceeded to take my formerly invincible self home and to bed. I ended up not getting out of bed for the next two months. Depression hit me with full force, and

I felt myself sinking lower than ever. I cried every day of the summer of 2016. Each day felt more pointless than the last. Everything bored me. The only routine I remember maintaining was my evening prayer that I wouldn't have to wake up in the morning, and that I could just go to sleep forever. So many people cared, so many wanted to help, but nothing made any difference. That is, until one day, as the summer came to an end. What Maria told me then would change my life, and lay the groundwork for the first and most essential tool I went on to create for my course in self-leadership, and for this book: the stress map.

Now I'd like to take you back to the sentence that opened this book: *Sometimes you ask for things and then receive them — only not in the way you expected!* I work as an international lecturer, coach and educator. Until this point in time, I had dedicated my whole adult life to my field, which is communication based on neuroscience, biology and psychology. Along with my team, I have spent seven years studying 5,000 lecturers, presenters and moderators to identify 110 different ways in which we all communicate. I spent two years writing 'The 110 Techniques of Communication and Public Speaking', the most viewed TEDx talk on storytelling of all time, where I deliberately triggered four specific neurotransmitters and hormones in my audience by telling different stories. My intention here isn't to present my CV to you in detail; rather, I want to emphasize that despite all these tools, techniques and methods, I had so far only managed to help my clients reach about seven out of ten. What was needed to reach level ten? I was giving them my all! It was all terribly frustrating. For almost ten years I had been roaming the world, searching for the key that would let me help the people I lectured to, trained and coached to truly maximize their potential. Despite this, the success I knew to be possible eluded me. At least, until I found that key where I least expected it.

It wasn't hidden in some book or in the possession of some specialist – it was within me. Now, I'm not suggesting it was there all along, or that I had actually been where I needed to be in order to find it. In my case, I needed to go through more than a decade of despair, recurring suicidal impulses, a summer of crying in absolute darkness, and then, five minutes of happiness on a bridge before the key would be revealed to me – rising from the waters like Excalibur. I didn't even realize that I had found it.

So let's return to that bridge, and those five minutes of happiness. It was like seeing colours, or perceiving smells, for the very first time. I'm sure you can imagine how motivated I was to re-experience that sensation once it had passed. It lit a spark in me, or, rather, it triggered a volcanic eruption. There was simply no stopping me after that! I remember running to my office after we returned from our walk, to jot down everything I had been doing recently that could possibly have caused it. I brought out the tool that can solve any problem in the world – Excel – and I wrote down all the things I had done, how much of each one I had done and when I had done it. That spark, predictably, triggered my energetic, manic side, and I barely slept for five days. During that time, I read countless research studies and books on the subject, brainstormed on whiteboards, took notes and made detailed schedules in Excel.

When I did occasionally manage to go to sleep, I invariably woke an hour or so later, only to continue my frenzied studies into self-leadership. Five days later, I had produced what would become my salvation, the recipe for my 'life 2.0'.

Over the next few months, I continued practising, and a month or so later, lightning struck again, and I experienced ten minutes of happiness, which would soon be followed by twenty, forty and even sixty minutes. The minutes turned into hours, the hours turned into days, and the following January, six months or so after my epiphany on the bridge, the balance shifted, and I experienced as many bright moments as I had previously had dark ones. That year was the best I've ever had. It was like being handed the keys to a magical wonderland. Everything seemed like an endless succession of tingling excitement and tears of joy.

Being a curious sort, I began to coach my clients to use the techniques I had been applying to myself, and that's when it happened: I realized, on a fully conscious level this time, that I had finally found what I had spent so much of my life looking for. The clients I coached and trained made quicker progress, and reached their absolute potential as leaders, teachers, doctors, speakers or salespeople. But that wasn't all. I also discovered that they were growing as individuals and fellow human beings in their personal lives. They were actually reaching level ten. My own insights had helped other people! This key, or, rather, these keys, are what I intend to give you here. You'll read about my experiences, the lessons I've learned from the tens of thousands of people I have coached and taught self-leadership to in every part of the world, and the studies that much of this journey is based on.

My promise to you, dear reader, is that if you use the most important techniques and tools in this book, and take the time to practise and apply them every day, within six months you'll experience a version of yourself and the world that you haven't been in touch with for a long time, if ever.

I'll mention the concept of self-leadership a fair number of times in the coming pages, and that's what this book is essentially about: learning to lead yourself – learning to choose your own emotions, and your own states, whenever you need or want to. If, for example, you're about to head into a meeting where you'll need to be decisive, the outcome of the meeting might well hinge on how much confidence you can bring to it. In terms of the six substances I go on to discuss, that would mean that the outcome depends on whether you choose to raise or lower your testosterone and dopamine levels before joining the meeting.

Now, you might be wondering how self-leadership relates to ordinary leadership. Have you ever met somebody who exhibited truly impressive self-leadership, i.e. somebody who could choose to always be their best self, in every situation, for you, for other people and for themselves? Somebody with that degree of self-knowledge and self-leadership will almost automatically become a natural leader in any group. People follow them because they want to, not because they have to. The opposite of this is somebody who lacks self-leadership, and whose emotions are all over the place. A person who *reacts* rather than *acts*. This kind of person will often create a lot of anxiety in others, and the people who follow them do so not because they want to, but because they have to.

PART ONE

An Angel's Cocktail, Please!

You sit up on the bar stool. Its worn leather bears witness to the many thoughts that various individuals have tried to dull with alcohol over the years, as well as probably to a small number of celebrations. The smell is the same as that of many other bars: a little acrid and a little old.

You lean across the bar and soon gain the bartender's attention. 'An Angel's cocktail, please!'

The bartender looks up at you with curiosity in her eyes. 'Exciting! They're all the rage. What would you like in it?'

You tell her that you'd like some motivation and a mood boost. 'I'll have dopamine and serotonin, please.'

After a while, she returns with your glass, which she has ceremoniously placed on a golden tray. It's a beautiful Martini glass, with a cocktail and a wooden stick that is piercing not the green olive you might have expected but a piece of fresh yellow pineapple. 'Enjoy your drink!'

Imagine if it could be that easy to change the way we feel! Imagine if all you needed to do was leave your home for a nearby bar, order the specific feeling you wanted, pay some money, make a toast and then wander home again with a new feeling in your body! Now imagine if it could be even simpler than that! Imagine having a chemical plant inside your brain that can produce six substances that you can use at will to manufacture the specific feeling you want, when you want it – all for free! Well, that's exactly what you do have. That's also the specific knowledge I want to give you in this book; I want to turn you into your own bartender, so that you can decide how to feel whenever you want. When do you want to be energized and full of dopamine? When do you want to be fully present and full of oxytocin? When do you want to be at ease and full of serotonin? When do you want to be euphoric and full of endorphins? And when do you want to be confident and full of testosterone?

Strangely enough, or perhaps not so strangely, there are a lot more people in our society who choose to mix up and guzzle down a *Devil's cocktail* instead, which in the context of this metaphor means exposing themselves to prolonged intense stress, ideally preceded by anxiety, disappointment and rumination. This state is often described as living in emotionless shades of grey – like inhabiting a surreal bubble, in which each day is much like the last, and life just carries on without any major eruptions of joy. However, consuming too many Devil's cocktails over too long a period can cause this state to escalate into dysphoria, anxiety and extended depression. One might very well ask why people choose to drink these Devil's cocktails. As I see it, there are three main reasons for this (although others exist too, of course):

- The first reason is that they were never taught any better. Our schools never seem to address these subjects, which are perhaps the most important lessons we can learn about life: what is an emotion, which emotions am I experiencing, how do they function and, most importantly, how can I learn to influence them? Our emotions impact everything we do, which makes this knowledge far more important than any of the subjects we're taught in school.

- The second reason is the society we've created, in which success is measured in money, and a constant quest for more takes priority over restful contentedness.
- The third reason is that we become like the people we surround ourselves with. If your friends are downing Devil's cocktails every day by exposing themselves to stress, pressure, bad news, comparisons with others, the constant hunt for more, and experiencing only infrequent moments of satisfaction, don't be surprised if your situation ends up similar. It works a bit like second-hand smoking.

When I managed to overcome my gloomy condition, the knowledge I had gained about my emotions and their origins in our biology and neuroscience was absolutely vital to my progress. But even if you feel OK, or even great, this book will still provide you with a useful and eye-opening perspective on life that will inform you in your roles as human being, leader, partner, friend or parent. In every course I give, at least one of the participants invariably says something along the lines of 'Imagine having to go through half a lifetime before even getting to learn what an emotion is, and that we can actually choose them for ourselves!' On one particular occasion, somebody else said, 'It's like watching colour TV for the first time.' They were both in tears when they said this. However, the comments that impact me the most are the ones I receive from parents. Most recently it was from Joakim, a father whose six-year-old Theodor was going through a period of rage that he was having a hard time getting over. His dad explained to him that emotions can be conjured up by thoughts, and that we're able to choose our thoughts. He suggested that they try a different thought together. Theodor gave him an enthusiastic look and agreed. Just minutes later, he was flashing a wide grin, and telling his dad, 'Look, look, it worked! Look at me, Dad! Look how happy I am!' Take inspiration from Theodor and his dad, and teach your kids and teenagers the things you learn from this book. Imagine what the world would be like if we could all understand that we aren't our emotions – rather, our emotions are largely temporary ideas that we have about ourselves and the world, ideas that we're actually free to choose!

These emotions, which we're generally able to choose by means of our thoughts, are primarily produced by a process in which substances called neuromodulators 'nudge' specific neurons in different directions, which in turn produces our experiences of having different emotions. But there's a lot more involved besides neuromodulators. In total, you have about fifty hormones and a hundred neurotransmitters working away in your body, and there are plenty of books and articles that describe all the substances we know the most about in minute detail. I can definitely recommend taking a deep dive into the world of biochemistry – it can even be more exciting than the latest bestselling murder mystery! However, this book isn't intended for people who are looking to spend a lot of time on detailed academic explorations of the various scientific discoveries that have been made. This is a pop-science book, and it was written to give a simplified account that can help everybody understand how our biochemistry can affect us, and how we can affect it in turn. When you let things get too complicated, you run the risk of making the knowledge you want to communicate intimidating rather than inviting. This subject has too often been discussed in inaccessible ways, but now that I've seen first-hand the effect this material has had on the tens of thousands of people I have trained, I feel encouraged to try to correct that. It's time this knowledge was made accessible to all. I want this to be a simple, digestible book about the most important thing in your life: your emotions. If you feel the urge to deepen or broaden your understanding of the things I discuss here, there is a hefty list of references and further reading at the end.

Now, if there are hundreds of substances involved, why have I chosen to write about just six? Well, I had three clear requirements for including a substance.

1. Each substance had to produce immediately noticeable effects.
2. Each substance had to be subject to voluntary production on your part, whenever you want it.

3. Each substance had to be accessible through the use of a simple, practical tool.

This is why the other 150 or so other substances didn't make the cut, where the absolute majority can't produce noticeable mental effects on demand. For example, oestrogen and progesterone, irrespective of their importance to all humans, aren't included, as they didn't fulfil all three criteria.

To make this book easier for you to use in practice, I've also chosen to only indicate the most significant mental effect of the six substances for each activity. In any given activity you'll see it's almost always the case that more than one of the six substances will be released together. However, they won't be released equally or produce equally significant mental effects. Perhaps you'll want to experience human closeness, and try to get a hug from a loved one. This would trigger the release of both oxytocin and dopamine, but it was the oxytocin you were specifically after (human closeness). In that case, it is the oxytocin that produces the most important effect, and that's why I've structured this book as I have.

Finally, but importantly, before we begin our journey together let me explain why Part Two is perhaps the most important. Part One covers your physiology and neurochemistry and the ways you can use these six substances to mix yourself an Angel's cocktail whenever and wherever you want to. The effects you will experience from your Angel's cocktail, however, will be temporary. These temporary effects will be useful to you in meetings, on dates, during presentations and in other situations. At best, the effect will last for a couple of hours – on a few rare occasions it might last for a day or two. That, you see, is where Part Two comes in. Although it is shorter than Part One, it is not to be underestimated; its contents are fundamental. There I'll explain how you can use repetition and neuroplasticity to bring about more permanent changes in yourself and mix up a cocktail that won't need refilling – its effects will stay with you! The two parts combined will give you all the priceless knowledge you need to grow and develop your personality in ways you've probably never imagined you could. And, as a massive cherry on top, I'll also teach you how to mix up an Angel's cocktail for others, a skill that will benefit you in both your leadership and your most important personal relationships.

To make sure you don't find this book overwhelming, I'd like to emphasize that the idea isn't for you to spend every waking moment meditating, exercising, observing a healthy diet, producing endorphins, taking cold-water baths, looking at pictures of your children, practising gratitude meditations, enjoying a minimum of 19 per cent deep sleep each night, varying your diet to enrich your microbial flora and being generous to everyone you meet. It's better to approach this book as an encyclopaedia, a handbook or a buffet. I recommend that you pick one or a few suggestions in it from time to time and practise them, so that slowly and gradually they can become automatic components of your overall lifestyle.

Just to be clear, the methods and tools in this book will help make you a better version of yourself. The insights and knowledge I teach here have the potential to change your life in fundamental ways. But be that as it may — if you're feeling too miserable, facing serious health struggles or battling depression, you should always get help from a healthcare professional.

Let's do this!

Dopamine

Drive and Pleasure

It's time to introduce our first amazing substance, dopamine.

Imagine waking up in the morning feeling like this: *I want to do this, it's going to be great, I can't wait!* You might head straight for the shower and then toss some clothes on, to kick-start the day as quickly as possible. The feeling you're experiencing is the sensation of a natural flow of dopamine. And it certainly *is* wonderful to feel like a rampant wild horse jubilantly greeting the coming spring!

Imagine being able to produce that feeling on command and being able to control it so that you could have more of it, with greater intensity, for longer periods of time. That's exactly what you're about to learn. Your life will probably never be the same again after you've read this chapter. You'll find yourself wanting to do things differently once you realize what incredible power properly directed dopamine can grant you. If dopamine is misdirected, however, it can produce emptiness, irritability, frustration, addiction and depression. Fortunately all you need in order to avoid that is some knowledge and the desire to do so.

Let's begin our dopamine exploration by gaining some understanding of the evolutionary purpose of dopamine. Our journey begins in a simple hut made from mammoth tusks, tree branches and clay. It's an entirely average Tuesday 25,000 years ago. An ancestor of yours – let's call him Duncan – is sleeping on his straw bed when he is awakened by a merciless sunbeam. The fact that the sun woke him rather than his rumbling stomach is something of a mystery really, but the moment he's fully awake he notices that he feels extremely hungry. After some thought, he realizes that he has nothing edible in the hut, but he knows of a marsh not too far away where juicy golden cloudberries grow. The mere thought of them releases dopamine in his brain, and he immediately feels a heightened sense of focus and drive.

The way there is difficult and involves contending with a fair deal of scrub, but by keeping those cloudberries at the top of his mind, he maintains his high dopamine levels, making him sufficiently energized to keep going. After a while, he finally arrives at a hilltop that gives him a good view of the barren bog. He desperately scans the ground for the golden berries he's looking for, but they've all been picked. His dopamine comes crashing down, and the pain of unfulfilled expectation arrives instead. With a sigh, Duncan sits down on a fallen tree, feeling a dreadful emptiness inside. How will he survive? He needs food! At that very moment he spots an apple in a tree. His spark reignites, and his dopamine gushes forth once more.

That apple *will* be his! After an adventurous climb over branches and rocks, he finally reaches his prize. He sits down and bites into the delicious wild apple. Duncan goes on to enjoy a reward cocktail mixed from elevated blood sugar, reduced stress and a dose of dopamine. This all makes

Duncan feel fantastic but unfortunately it only lasts for a short while. To encourage Duncan to look for more apples, his brain reduces his dopamine levels, lowering them to even further than they were before he found the apple. The sudden feeling of emptiness Duncan experiences in the absence of dopamine will motivate him to look for more apples. It will also spur him on to gather food for the winter, finish building his hut and invest effort in making his straw bed a little softer and more comfortable. He's driven by the desire to improve his circumstances and achieve progress that will help him survive and pass on his genes.

Now let's fast-forward 25,000 years to the present day. You're not really that hungry, but you realize that you'd very much enjoy some ice cream, sweets and crisps. You get in your car and drive what seems like rather a long way to do some shopping. When you arrive, the shop has closed, and you experience a new emptiness, a hole inside you that cries out to be filled. You drive to another shop but it's closed too, which only strengthens your resolve – you're determined now to find a shop that's open. And, lo and behold, the next shop *is* open! The satisfaction you feel from your dopamine surge is enormous. Any moment now you'll be . . . But then disaster strikes. You left your money at home! Your dopamine comes crashing back down and it stays horribly low until you find your wallet, which was actually in the car all along. What a relief! You pay and can hardly wait to get home – if we're being honest, you probably start snacking while you're still in the car. You eat a little more, relishing your snacks, and keep going until you run out. Soon, however, you don't feel so great any more. What's happened is that your dopamine has dropped down below your baseline, i.e. the level it was at before you headed out to the shop. This sudden emptiness that a reduction in dopamine can cause in us will make us seek it elsewhere – from our smartphone's delightful dopamine-inducing apps or from a TV show perhaps. This cycle can turn us into constant pleasure-seekers, eternally on the hunt for dopamine. Duncan was just like that, but in his case, it helped him gather a supply of apples, fix his hut up for the winter and make his bed more comfortable.

While our biological reward system hasn't changed much in 25,000 years, the society we've created certainly has. In our world there is an abundance of dopamine sources that didn't exist back then. In Duncan's days the purpose of dopamine was to produce circumstances that were more likely to promote survival. Please don't think that I'm in any way suggesting we shouldn't be enjoying any of the 'unnecessary' dopamine sources that keep us going – I'm not! I watch TV shows, I enjoy a bit of ice cream from time to time and I certainly indulge in popcorn when I watch movies. What I *am* suggesting, rather, is that understanding how dopamine works is an essential survival skill, particularly in a society such as ours, in which dopamine thieves – which I'll return to in a moment – lurk around every corner.

So what does dopamine do for us? As a component of an Angel's cocktail, dopamine produces motivation, momentum, desire and pleasure, as well as playing an important role in our acquisition of long-term memories. Technically there are four dopaminergic brain pathways, but we'll only focus on two here: the one that regulates rewards, and the one that regulates executive functions like willpower and decision-making.

Let's return to an important concept: the dopamine baseline. Andrew D. Huberman, professor and brain researcher at Stanford University, has given a brilliant explanation of this. To get us to make more effort on searching, learning and making progress, dopamine levels increase before and during all those activities, only to be reduced to a level below the baseline we had before after the activity. Let's use a scale from 1 to 10 to illustrate this. Every individual's baseline is unique – in part, this is an innate trait. In this example, though, the baseline is 5. Suppose you do something that causes your level to rise, like watching a fun video on Instagram, which elevates your dopamine level to 6. Immediately after you finish watching the clip, your dopamine will drop to 4.9, to encourage you to 'keep searching'. So you watch another clip, which you enjoy just as much as the first one, but since you started out at a lower level (4.9), you only reach 5.9 this time, and then drop back down to 4.8. It goes on like this, clip after clip, until you lose interest in the videos, because you're no longer finding them as entertaining as you did when you began. Your baseline has dropped to 4, and objectively you feel worse than you did when you started browsing your feed.

Now you've probably experienced exceptions to this rule first-hand. Sometimes the dopamine effect will actually leave us *more* energized and positive afterwards. So what causes this difference? Well, if your feed of video clips consists exclusively of genuinely motivating materials, you'll feel more energized than before. Think of this as two different kinds of dopamine: fast and slow dopamine. I want to be clear: there's really no such thing as 'fast' or 'slow' dopamine. What I'm referring to is the effects of the released dopamine, which can either be long-lasting or short-lasting. This is similar to the concept of slow and fast carbohydrates. Fast carbs, which you get from white bread, pasta and sugar, give you a rapid energy boost, which is soon followed by a crash. Think of the Instagram videos. Slow carbs, which you get from brown bread, lentils, brown rice and grains, on the other hand, give you long-lasting energy. So what triggers slow dopamine? The answer is activities and experiences that will be of use to you in the future, whose benefits extend beyond the present moment. Let's repeat this point – it's an important one: slow dopamine is characterized by activities and experiences that will actually be of use to you in the future, whose benefits extend beyond the present moment. According to this definition, most of the things our ancestors experienced provided slow dopamine.

Let's examine some examples of slow dopamine.

Watching videos that educate, energize or motivate you can potentially feed you long-term fuel! It can spark the desire or longing to change or create something in you. It can help you make progress in your life. The opposite, however, would be scrolling past hundreds of clips that offer nothing but momentary entertainment, which leaves you feeling empty when you're done.

Reading fiction is clearly a slow dopamine activity, as the effects of reading last far longer than the momentary experience of doing it. Among other things, it trains your eye muscles, your imagination and large portions of your brain when you simulate the events in the book in your head. It also engages your memory, because you need to remember the events and characters until your next reading session.

Learning things produces slow dopamine. Knowledge trains your memory. New knowledge fosters creativity, because a new idea is always, invariably, some combination or other of old ideas. Knowledge helps you to better understand the world. Knowledge also allows you to communicate with others in a variety of social situations. Also, the greater your knowledge, the more knowledge of similar kinds you'll be able to associate with it and hold on to.

Physical exercise releases slow dopamine. In fact, exercise produces an almost infinite set of benefits, but here are some highlights: exercise reduces your risk of suffering cardiovascular disease, boosts your energy, improves your sleep, increases your neuroplasticity (see page 215 for further discussion on this topic), strengthens your immune system and is thought to be the single most important contributor to positive mental well-being.

Sex also releases slow dopamine. The 'benefit' of consensual sex is that it improves both your own and your partner's perceptions of your relationship for forty-eight hours. Sex is a form of cardiovascular exercise and can produce an outstanding Angel's cocktail in its own right, because it also raises your serotonin and oxytocin levels.

In my lectures, I often state, jokingly, that most things we did before commercial television entered our lives were good sources of slow dopamine. When I ask my audience what they imagine people used to do more of before television adverts and the internet invaded their lives, these are some of the responses I tend to get: socializing, spending time on hobbies, cooking meals at home, reading books and magazines, playing board games, DIY projects, gardening, dancing, being creative and making things, solving crosswords. And then somebody always gets a laugh with this one: 'We used to listen to the whole album in one go!' And, yes, we actually did do that. There was a time when bringing a new album home and putting it in our CD player was almost a sacred ritual. We made sure to turn off all distractions first, and then just listened, one song after another.

But that was a long time ago. We live in a new world now, a world that runs on fast dopamine. This is the source of many of our problems. The main challenge here is that sources of slow dopamine often demand more energy and active management of us than sources of fast dopamine. You can easily feed yourself fast dopamine by just crashing out on the couch and stuffing yourself with chocolate (an activity that can raise dopamine to 150 per cent of the baseline level). Other fast-dopamine sources include junk food, TV series, smartphone games, social media, frequent checking of bitcoin rates or stock prices, and the news. Slow dopamine, on the other hand, often requires a larger – sometimes much larger – investment. For example, working on your hobby, solving a crossword or playing a board game all require more time and energy. And if there's one thing the human brain hates, it's expending any more energy than is absolutely necessary. Energy, without a doubt, is the most valuable currency in all evolution!

A fun energy study you can conduct the next time you're in a shopping mall is seeing how many people choose the escalators as opposed to the stairs. My own nerdy observations, which I've made notes of when sitting in mall cafés, have shown me that the absolute majority of people will always choose escalators over stairs, even when descending a floor, which makes zero rational sense when you consider how aware most of us are of the health benefits of exercise. However, from an evolutionary point of view, it makes perfect sense. For Duncan, preserving energy meant that he needed less food, and the more food he was able to save, the fewer dangers he would have to expose himself to by going out to gather more of it. Other examples of everyday energy preservation that we tend to indulge in include:

- Taking the car rather than cycling or walking
- Taking the car rather than using public transport
- Riding an electric scooter rather than using public transport
- Getting a takeaway rather than cooking a meal
- Texting someone rather than talking to them
- Using moving walkways in airports rather than walking
- Using a riding mower or robotic mower rather than manually mowing the lawn

Naturally it could be argued that these activities allow us to spend more time doing things we actually enjoy, but more often than not we make these choices subconsciously, in accordance with our primordial instinct to preserve energy.

If you develop an addiction to activities that provide fast dopamine, you'll soon be mixing yourself a proper Devil's cocktail. Overindulgence can cause you to distance yourself from slow-dopamine sources and avoid activities that would benefit you in the long term. A secondary effect of readily accessible dopamine is the development of tolerance, which causes you to need more stimulation to achieve the same enjoyable effect. You've probably witnessed first-hand somebody watching YouTube while playing video games, eating snacks and enjoying some kind of drink all at once; this constitutes a stacking of four simultaneous dopamine sources. Making this person sit through the movie classic *Casablanca* without any auxiliary dopamine sources would probably be their equivalent of torture. It's worth considering that the same film made whole cinema theatres gasp for breath in 1942, as at the time it was considered an extremely exciting and emotionally overwhelming picture. Mastering dopamine stacking is a vital skill for a successful life, and a necessary step towards any healthy Angel's cocktail – we'll return to this in a moment. Before we do, though, let's get back to the lurking dopamine thieves.

What are they, and where do we encounter them? The truth is, they're all around you. They can even get between you and the people you love the most. Businesses have realized that they can monetize your time, or rather your dopamine. Let's take a single example, a company that makes a game app. This company now has three ways to make money off you:

- The more time they can demonstrably get you to spend on their app or website, the more ad revenue they can generate from their advertising clients
- The more time they can make you want to spend on their app, the more likely it is that you'll be prepared to spend money on upgrades and updates
- The more users they can harvest dopamine from, the more users they will have, and the greater the perceived value of their app, website or business

Their whole business idea, then, aims at triggering the maximum possible amount of dopamine in you, and then converting your response into money. In developing these gaming and gambling apps, some companies have even conducted in-depth studies of cognition, psychology and biology to learn how to maximize fast dopamine through the use of colours, sounds, shapes and animations. But why don't they focus on slow dopamine instead, and provide actual value and long-term benefit to their customers? Well, for one thing, if they did that, they would fall victim to the 'escalator phenomenon'. The dopamine thieves are offering you an escalator. If somebody else were to suddenly offer you a physical staircase, they would be asking you to invest a lot more energy, and, as I've mentioned, we've evolved to avoid that.

Dopamine thieves don't only lurk in your smartphone. How do manufacturers get you to buy their products in shops? Well, they make them seem more appealing than other products. How do they do that? They start by making the product appear tastier, by giving its packaging a mouth-watering design. Why not make it satisfying to touch too? This will raise your expectations and cause your fast dopamine to spike. Suddenly your attention will be drawn to a brand-new variety of some product or other, a variety you've never tried before, and your dopamine will rise even more. You go home, open the packaging and try the product, which promised to be a healthy breakfast option. Your dopamine will spike even more when the 15 per cent sugar the product contains reaches your bloodstream. Your brain will be in bliss at this point, and you'll quickly internalize the lesson that this is a wonderful product that you'll be buying again. A moment later, your dopamine baseline will drop, and your brain will start screaming about how it doesn't want to feel this way. *Feed me more dopamine!*

Nobody likes stealing, especially not from children. There's even an expression, 'like stealing candy from a baby'. The modern version of this really ought to be 'like stealing dopamine from a baby'. The way apps and games are specifically designed to trigger maximal amounts of dopamine in children is genuinely horrific! At least grown-ups are theoretically able to resist them. Our brains' prefrontal cortexes are far more developed, and this gives us a much greater ability to think rationally and exhibit willpower than children or teenagers. Adults have a much easier time choosing slow dopamine over fast dopamine. However, despite this, many adults still fall victim to dopamine thieves. If you get caught up in that cycle, you could end up with a gradually deteriorating dopamine baseline, which will make it increasingly difficult for you to experience pleasure and genuine motivation, which, in turn, can cause feelings of emptiness, dysphoria and possibly even depression.

Are there no positives to fast dopamine? There certainly are. Fast dopamine is an important component of our pleasure, and part of what makes life so magical. Of course we should eat chocolate, enjoy a glass of wine, eat dessert, play video games, watch TV and use dating apps; I do myself, and none of you should have to go without! But ideally you should enjoy these things only when the following two conditions are fulfilled:

1. You are aware of the effects of fast dopamine, and the way it can distract you from slower dopamine.
2. You have learned to handle dopamine. The problem is, if you don't own your dopamine, it will end up owning you.

So let's do precisely that: learn how to better handle fast dopamine. I'm about to give you six tools that you can use to rein in and master your own fast dopamine, and thus preserve your natural inclination to add more 'real activities' to your life. You're in for quite a ride, I can tell you! I'll close this chapter with another four tools that you can use to produce dopamine and motivation on demand whenever you need to. Remember to go slow with this stuff, and make sure to find time to reflect on how each tool impacts your life.

Tool 1: Dopamine Stacking

1. Does the following scenario sound familiar to you? When the dopamine we get from watching a TV series on the computer isn't enough, we add some popcorn; when that's not enough, we add a drink; when that's not enough, we browse our smartphones at the same time; and, when *that's* not enough, we put the TV on in the background. We stack dopamine sources on top of one another. This can cause three different problems. The first is that there is no natural end to the stacking – you'll find yourself needing to stack more and more dopamine sources to achieve the same satisfying effects.

2. The second problem is that our brains will always want to indulge in stacking, which means that when we're in sensitive situations, like when we're driving, the brain will still demand we do it, and we'll be far more prone to succumbing to the urge to browse our phones when that's the very last thing we ought to be doing. Car accidents, for example, have become 10–30 per cent more frequent in various regions of the world as a direct consequence of smartphone use.

3. The third and final problem stacking can cause is that it makes it more difficult for us to appreciate and enjoy the original activity we were engaging in – watching a TV series, for example.

So how should we address this? Awareness of the phenomenon of dopamine stacking can be enough to make you start doing something about it. However, if you feel that you need to take stronger measures, I have three approaches you might try:

1. Cease all stacking immediately and get disciplined about limiting yourself to a single activity at a time. For example, watch a TV show without any distractions, focus on spending time with your children or just drive the car without making a phone call or listening to a podcast.
2. Eliminate one dopamine source at a time from your stack: put your phone away completely when you watch TV, turn the TV that's running in the background off and so on.
3. Go *cold turkey*. During my years as a self-leadership coach, I've received plenty of feedback regarding the wonderful benefits of eliminating all sources of fast dopamine for anywhere from ten to thirty days. Clients have described picking up their smartphones thirty days later and marvelling at how they spent so much time on it before, as though they had been under some spell or hypnotized. A tip for anybody interested in going cold turkey or trying

an intermediate approach in which you remove half of all the fast dopamine in your life is to replace what you eliminate with slow-dopamine sources. Start reading books, solving crosswords, socializing, revisiting an abandoned hobby or something along those lines – it'll make the transition a lot smoother. I'm not suggesting, as is fashionable, that you go through a 'dopamine detox'. Dopamine is not a toxin. Your brain has simply developed the habit of satisfying its dopamine cravings quickly, and habits are something our brains tend to cling to, as they are highly energy efficient.

Tool 2: Dopamine Balancing

When there is an imbalance between our fast and slow dopamine, this can affect our everyday lives. One lesson I have learned from the courses I've taught is that this balance is highly individual. My definition of dopamine balance is simply the ratio between fast and slow dopamine that you allow into your life. Personally I try to maintain something like an 80/20 balance, which seems to be the sweet spot for most people. This means that I can fill my waking hours with about 20 per cent fast dopamine without those dopamine sources threatening to control my days or steer me away from slower dopamine. If I feed myself 40 per cent fast dopamine at the weekend, my brain will tend to seek to avoid anything involving slower dopamine, like gardening, DIY projects or exercise.

A great strategy here is to refrain from starting your day by checking your phone, as the fast dopamine you're likely to receive will make you less 'hungry' for slower dopamine. According to Dr Nikole Benders-Hadi, the jarring transition from the state of sleep to the massive information input your phone feeds you also tends to impact your ability to focus and prioritize for the rest of the day. Give it a try for a few mornings and experience the difference it makes.

Another tip is to turn off the notifications on your phone. For somebody with a dopamine craving, notifications can be the equivalent of waving a bag of crisps in front of a hungry person. As soon as you look at a single notification (eat a single crisp), you'll develop an even stronger urge to check your phone a moment later (eat more crisps).

Tool 3: Intermittent Dopamine

Allowing yourself fast dopamine at any time, in any circumstances, will have an adverse effect on your ability to enjoy life. Let's examine a familiar example from the world of music. The first time you listen to a new song, you might find yourself thinking, *Wow, this is really good!* After this, the song will seem better and better each time you listen to it. Essentially, listening to the song is consistently feeding you greater and greater amounts of dopamine, until one day, when you find that you're not getting the same satisfaction from that song any more. A few months later, you might even find yourself feeling rather tired of it. If, instead, you had portioned out your dopamine, by letting more time pass between each listen, the song might have lasted longer for you. Another example of this is *binge-watching*, where you watch an entire TV series in one sitting. This is like downing a whole bag of sweets in one go. It'll feel wonderful initially, but your enjoyment won't last very long. Once the whole thing ends, a dopamine crash is sure to follow. Personally I love to make a TV series last, and I try to go as long as I possibly can before watching the next episode. This approach really gives a huge dopamine boost. After I watch an episode, I get to spend time enjoying my memories of it, as well as my musings and speculations as I think about the characters and imagine what might happen next. Then, just when my brain shows signs of losing interest, I watch the next episode. That way, I can enjoy a TV series or novel for a long time. I've even refrained from watching the last episodes of some TV series entirely, because I enjoy the dopamine release I get from imagining what the conclusion might be. OK, I'll admit to being something of a geek when it comes to intermittent dopamine dosing, but I'm sure I'm not the only one.

Another thing, which I know for a fact I'm not the only one who enjoys, is the 'purchase dance', i.e. the occasionally subconscious but usually entirely conscious process people go through before buying something. It's when you allow yourself to savour the hunt for the perfect purchase by exploring options, reading, studying, researching and asking questions about whatever it is you want to buy. The whole pre-purchase dance can produce a highly pleasurable experience. Portioning your dopamine is simply a way of making the experience last. The opposite of this approach is to buy the thing right away, and enjoy a huge dopamine boost that will invariably be followed by a rapid crash.

Now, while we're on the topic of crashes, perhaps it's worth asking if we can make something good out of them too. Yes, you can learn to portion the crash itself, at least in some situations. Imagine working on a project with a deadline, and reaching the finishing line after months of hard, anxious efforts. You're likely to feel absolutely terrific, and will probably invite the whole team to celebrate the project's completion. Everybody will be there, and the mood will be sky-high! The next day, though, it's time to start the next project. Four months of hard work won you four hours of celebrations – now, tell me, does that seem reasonable to you? You're practically asking for a dopamine crash. You might try to avoid this by launching the next project immediately; however, this is not a sustainable long-term approach to work. My advice: portion out your celebrations! Enjoy your successes for longer. Celebrate all week long, but with less intensity on each individual day. Share your memories of the project and talk about your successes. This will also win you an interesting positive side effect: you and your team will find yourself more motivated to take on the next project!

Tool 4: Intrinsic vs Extrinsic Dopamine

David Greene and Mark R. Lepper of Stanford University conducted an incredibly exciting, albeit somewhat sadistic, experiment on a preschool class. Like many other children, the subjects were given opportunities to draw at their preschool, and they loved doing it. They had what is referred to as *intrinsic motivation*. This means that they were motivated by the very process of drawing: it made them feel good, they could see their work progress and they enjoyed doing it. In the next phase of the experiment, the children began to receive awards for their drawings, which introduced an extrinsic dopamine source. The children would receive one of these awards every time they made a drawing, and at first they were delighted whenever they got one. However, one day, the researchers stopped handing out these extrinsic rewards, and, as a result, the preschool children showed significantly less interest in drawing. They stopped doing it, as their previous intrinsic motivation to draw had been replaced by an extrinsic one, which had subsequently been removed. Both their motivational sources were now gone.

This tool is an incredibly important one to apply in your own life. The trick here is to make the process itself the motivator. In other words, the reward you receive after you do something shouldn't be what's providing your motivation. You might feel low on motivation to go to the gym and decide to reward yourself with a smoothie or energy drink afterwards. This extrinsic reward structure could end up leaving you with even less natural and intrinsic motivation to get your exercise done. Instead, you should try to remove that extrinsic reward, and focus on how good it feels to exercise, how energized it makes you feel, the thrill of seeing your physique improve and so on. The same approach can be applied to raking leaves in the garden. Rather than thinking about how you'll reward yourself by listening to a podcast while you do it, or taking a nice hot bath afterwards, you should focus on how wonderful it is to be outside, how nice you're making the garden look, how beautifully the birds are singing or how pleasantly warm the autumn sun is!

The magical neurological explanation for why this works is that your prefrontal cortex (your willpower) tells you that you can find enjoyment in the process itself. Now, I'm not trying to suggest that using this tool is an all-or-nothing proposition. I *do* love to give myself little rewards for my achievements from time to time. *However*, I make sure not to let these rewards become more important to me than the pleasure I take from the activities themselves.

Tool 5: Dopamine Variability

This tool is inspired by games. There are many reasons why people will so gladly gamble and game their time and money away just for the thrill it gives them, and one of the tricks that encourage people to play more is to let them come excitingly close to winning. Almost winning gives you more dopamine than a defeat, and the feeling it gives you will encourage you to give the game another go. So how can this principle be put to use in your everyday life? Carry a die around or install a die-rolling app on your phone. The next time you set out to do something you do often, like getting a coffee at your favourite café, roll the die instead. If you get a one, you'll buy your coffee at a corner shop, if it's a two, you'll get it from the supermarket café and so on, and only if you get a six do you allow yourself to go to your favourite coffee shop. This 'game' can be simplified by using the rule that if you roll one to three, you get to do the thing you wanted to, and if you roll four to six, you don't get to do it. I once used this game, a long time ago, on a road trip with my cousin. We rolled the die at each fork in the road, going left on a one to three and right on a four to six. Now, although we did end up camping out on a mosquito-infested bog in the north of Sweden, it was still the most exciting trip I've ever taken!

One way that games grab your attention is by offering you surprises. If a game is predictable, and you can always tell exactly how it's going to end, you will invariably grow bored of it. This is also why so many food manufacturers spend so much time and effort introducing new products or changing the packaging for existing products. How, then, can you apply this to improve your life? In a study carried out by Ed O'Brien and Robert W. Smith, they asked test subjects to eat popcorn with chopsticks, which made the popcorn seem tastier, more flavourful and more fun to eat. They also had their subjects drink water from unconventional glassware, such as Martini glasses, which was also reported to increase their satisfaction. You've probably noticed this phenomenon yourself in the past. Doing something that might otherwise be commonplace in a new way can immediately make the whole experience more memorable and enjoyable, and thus more satisfactory on the whole.

Tool 6: Dopamine Hangover

The last of these tools is meant to be used as a helpful warning sign, as well as a cure you can use to alleviate an undesirable hangover. Who knows – perhaps dopamine hangovers are the most common variety of hangovers people suffer from these days? Amusingly this hangover tends to rear its head on Saturdays and Sundays, but it's *not* caused by an excessive intake of alcohol. What causes it is the huge contrast between the amounts of dopamine you've experienced during your busy and stimulating work week, and your sudden lack of dopamine at the weekend. It also happens the other way round in some cases; after a weekend of dopamine excess, Monday comes round, and it's time to return to a job you don't enjoy, which gives you very little in the way of dopamine. Many will self-medicate with binge-watching or spending time on their phones. Some do this wisely, in moderation, as a means of recovery, while others are merely indulging in escapism. For some, the sudden emptiness and dopamine abstinence can present as dysphoria or sadness, while others might respond with anxiety and depression-like symptoms.

After reading this, you'll have the advantage of knowing

that a dopamine hangover is a thing, and that it can happen to all of us. If it's a pattern you recognize in yourself, you can choose to accept it rather than let it ruffle you – that alone can make a huge difference. The other insight I'd like to offer is that it's wise to avoid overdosing on fast dopamine at the weekend, because it can foster a need to constantly max out on dopamine, which is unhealthy in the long run. Instead, you should try to balance out your fast dopamine at the weekends by engaging in 'real activities' that will produce slow dopamine. Examples of the latter are going for walks, spending time in the sunshine, going to the gym, socializing, playing board games, reading books, meditating or resting.

What Happens When You Run Out of Dopamine?

If you subject your brain to an endless succession of dopamine spikes for years on end, this can cause the source to 'dry up'. To put this more precisely, you end up desensitizing yourself to dopamine, which involves a long-lasting reduction in dopamine signalling and receptor activity. A dulled reward response is probably the easiest way to identify an addiction.

Addictions tend to start out as small habits that gradually become increasingly difficult to control. We're all prone to various forms of addiction. You can prove this by visiting a cosy café. People have always sought out places like that to eat, socialize and talk to each other.

However, these days a social encounter with a friend over a sweet treat and a latte simply isn't enough for most people. Instead, almost everybody can be seen bringing their phone out every few seconds to give themselves an extra dopamine boost. Look around the next time you visit a café. Friends will often sit together, preoccupied with their phones instead of engaging with each other. Their reward responses have been dulled and dopamine stacking seems to be their only way to reach that seductive dopamine spike that they find increasingly difficult to achieve each day. It's not at all unfair to say that many of us have become dopamine junkies.

Another example of this would be somebody who has been working long and hard thanks to the powerful drive their dopamine gives them. Slowly, gradually, almost imperceptibly, their reward response will begin to fade, and they might start to use food and alcohol to achieve the same effects through dopamine stacking. Their stress levels will rise, and they will have to push themselves even harder to reach the dopamine high they crave, which in turn further exacerbates their stress and diminishes their pleasure (and dopamine), and they'll end up compensating for this with even more food and alcohol. It's a vicious cycle.

I remember a train trip I took to Malmö about ten years ago, before I had learned about dopamine stacking and the desensitization it can cause. Across the aisle from me, an older gentleman was looking out through the window at the countryside. I was sitting with my laptop, working and watching a movie. When the movie ended, I read the news on my phone and browsed through my social media feeds, and then ended up playing games until the battery went flat. At this point, I picked up *Kupé*, the complimentary magazine the Swedish railway used to provide for passengers on all their trains. I began reading it. I finished it. I found myself growing desperate for some entertainment, as my immediate, severe dopamine hangover raged through my body. Something inside me was crying out for *more*! But now that I was forced to focus on something other than my screens, I watched that older gentleman again. He had been sitting in his seat all along, with the same smile on his face, just watching the countryside rushing past the window for almost two hours. That was when I realized that I was a dopamine addict.

Your Dopamine Engine

Dopamine is your positive engine, the energy source that can help you finish any task, whether it be fun or difficult, with a smile and a great sense of satisfaction. These six tools will allow you to regain your primeval energy, your natural desire to do 'real things' in life, as well as help you handle fast dopamine. You'll soon be humming as gently as a well-oiled Rolls-Royce engine. However, engines can do more than hum; they can go fast too. The question that I've yet to answer is how we can 'inject' dopamine into ourselves on demand, to give ourselves an immediate boost of motivation to kick-start the day, our next project or our next activity. Here are four more dopamine tools that can help you do precisely that.

Tool 7: Emotional Whys

When my son Tristan was nine years old, and was supposed to be learning his times tables, he put up a lot of resistance. Nobody could make him sit down and learn them. That is, until my wife Maria opened a café during the summer of that year. Tristan saw an opportunity for some extra income to supplement his pocket money and asked his mother if she would let him work in the cafe. She replied, 'Absolutely. You can work at the counter and take payment from customers.' Being a rather social being, he was immediately thrilled at this idea. However, she went on to add the following: 'You'll need to learn your times tables first, though, because people often buy more than one of something, like three lollipops for 30p each.' Tristan soon understood why he needed to learn his times tables. His motivation was in place, and the rest, as they say, is history.

I personally use one of ten powerful 'whys', depending on which activity I need to charge my dopamine levels for. Here are four examples that I use to create a huge boost of motivation in under a minute:

1. If I'm feeling less than motivated to teach one of my self-leadership classes, I sit down and think about how it felt to struggle with depression for seventeen years, how much my life has changed since then and how I don't want anybody to ever have to feel the way I did.

43

2. If I'm feeling low on motivation to go to the gym, I think of my dad. He was British, a legendary character, who used to hang out with Sean Connery and Roger Moore, and who really deserved better than to spend the last fifteen years of his life suffering three strokes and having to deal with their dreadful consequences. His strokes were, in part, caused and exacerbated by his choices to not exercise properly or keep to a sensible diet. In this way, my father serves as my most powerful source of motivation, my strongest *why* for making sure I eat properly and go to the gym regularly.

3. If I'm lacking motivation to give my lecture 'How to Avoid Death by PowerPoint', I think of a meeting at my son's school, when his teacher brought up the most horrendous PowerPoint with a white background that was littered with microscopic text, turned the lights out, stood in the corner and spoke in a monotonous voice while flicking a red laser pointer about on the screen.

4. Being an introvert, I almost always find the prospect of meeting new people quite anxiety-inducing, and if I trusted my gut feeling, I'd simply cancel the meeting. Instead of doing that, I replace my sense of fear with a *why*, which involves focusing on how exciting the meeting will be and recalling all the magical encounters I've had with new people.

To make your *why* powerful enough to be useful for on-demand motivation, you should associate it with a specific emotion or memory – you've no doubt noticed that all my examples do this – and you can find your *whys* in negative memories as well as in positive ones. Once you've found your *why*, you need to recall the emotions you associate with it and increase their intensity until you can physically feel them coursing through your body. Some will find this easier to do than others, but everybody can do it.

You can also create emotional *whys* by exposing yourself to the specific situation or location that triggers your emotion. Here's an example: my children were incredibly keen on getting a pet rabbit – two ideally. However, they were having a difficult time saving the money they needed to buy the rabbits. I thought this was a shame, because keeping rabbits would be a good opportunity for them to practise maintaining a routine, nurture, empathy, respect and all the other things we learn by keeping pets. So I brought two baby rabbits home one weekend. On the Sunday I returned them to the breeder. This certainly kicked the kids into gear! They had been given a taste of their emotional *why*, and the impact was enormous. Three weeks later, they had made sure to earn the money in all kinds of ways, and we visited the breeder to buy the very rabbits we had borrowed that weekend. I'll admit that there was some friction when I returned the rabbits, but the method worked like a charm. If you want something, steep yourself in it, to give yourself a taste of the feeling you crave. This feeling will soon become your emotional *why* and a great source of motivation to get you to your goal.

Tool 8: Cold-Water Bathing

In a study orchestrated by the *European Journal of Applied Physiology*, participants who were asked to bathe in chilly 14-degree water for sixty minutes experienced a boost in their dopamine levels of up to 250 per cent. The increase was gradual – it didn't suddenly kick in after an hour – but even short periods of cold exposure will positively impact your dopamine and endorphin levels, resulting in a sustained elevation of mood, energy and increased focus. This increased focus is one effect of the noradrenaline that is generated by somebody who has exposed their body to the stress of a cold bath. And noradrenaline is a building block of – you guessed it! – dopamine!

Tool 9: The Vision Board

The power of the mind is far greater than most people realize. Just thinking of going on holiday can give you a tingle of excitement, right? The same applies to thinking of a new phone, car or coat you want to buy. Doesn't it feel nice, and doesn't it make you feel motivated to work for it? However, as soon as you begin thinking of something else, the dopamine you just felt will no longer exert the same pull on you. Since most of us tend to have less-than-perfect memories, a *vision board* is an essential tool for everybody.

You'll need a large sheet of paper, some colourful pens, a good pair of scissors and a frame. Stick pictures of your dreams and visions on to the paper. Write down phrases and quotes that remind you of who you want to be or what you want to create. Basically you're making a picture of the future you want for yourself. When you've finished, you should frame it and hang it on the wall of your bedroom or bathroom – or maybe the inside of your wardrobe door. Then spend some time each morning looking at your vision board, perhaps when you get out of bed or brush your teeth. Make sure to feel the feelings you've described on it and try to savour your dreams and your goals. This will feed you dopamine in real time. You'll literally feel your motivation grow and sense how you're becoming energized. A good trick is to choose one thing from your vision board to practise or focus particularly on each day. Take a photo of it and add it to your computer or phone's wallpaper or screensaver, so that you can feed yourself little doses of encouragement throughout the day, wherever you happen to be.

Tool 10: Momentum

Most of us are familiar with the mysterious aid that momentum can provide once we actually get going on something. When we've forced ourselves to go to the gym four times a week, we find ourselves saying we could keep it up forever. But eventually we get sick or go on holiday for a couple of weeks, and afterwards we can find it very difficult to get back on track. Momentum, basically, seems to produce its own dopamine.

If you go to the gym regularly for a while and start seeing results, this will strengthen your motivation to keep going. The good thing about this is that you can use this to feed your dopamine engine, by simply understanding what you need to do to get that feeling back – i.e. get started! Once you're up and running again, this is very likely to trigger a dopamine release, which in turn triggers more dopamine, and presto! The engine will be running itself again! But don't forget that dopamine has a short shelf life, and allowing too much time to go by between your activities can make you lose your momentum again. And, finally, your attitude to the activity itself will have a huge impact on how you experience it. Have you ever noticed that convincing yourself that a certain experience or activity is desirable, pleasurable or rewarding can help you achieve a greater sense of satisfaction and perhaps even greater drive?

Dopamine – A Summary

Your Angel's cocktail can be made up of two different varieties of dopamine. On the one hand, there's what I call 'fast dopamine', which I define as quick injections of dopamine that serve no real long-term purpose for you, like eating chocolate, absent-mindedly browsing your phone or eating a bag of crisps. Mix some fast dopamine in with your Angel's cocktail and allow yourself to enjoy the good things in life – I certainly do! However, you should avoid stacking these pleasures. A far better approach would be to portion them out: indulge in smaller doses and limit connecting your motivation to external rewards. On the other hand, there is the other variety, 'slow dopamine', which should be the main ingredient of your Angel's cocktail. I define this as those injections of dopamine that bring genuine benefit to you, either immediately or in the future. Examples of this include learning something new, exercising, being creative, socializing, solving crosswords and approaching challenges as opportunities for growth rather than problems to be overcome. If you reduce your intake of fast dopamine, you'll very soon see your natural desire for slow dopamine return. To add even more slow dopamine to your Angel's cocktail, you can identify your emotional *whys*, make a vision board, strive for momentum and take cold-water baths.

Oxytocin

Connectedness and Humanity

'Wow! Look at this magical sunset! Come here!' You're mesmerized, awestruck, and time stops for a moment. Your breathing relaxes, deepens and settles, and you feel an unexpected sense of harmony and well-being, even though the sky you're looking at is the very same one that you didn't even notice this morning. Your mood can be altered in this way by a beautiful flower, an incredible view or seeing your child walk for the very first time. What you're experiencing is the emotion of *awe*, which is the sensation of being humbled by greatness that can often seem magical. Awe is generally held to be in a class of its own among emotions. Awe triggers releases of serotonin and dopamine, but I've chosen to address it in this chapter on oxytocin, because oxytocin has the unique function of forging a sense of connectedness between yourself and others, between yourself and objects, or between yourself and something greater. The last is often caused by experiences related to nature, the cosmos or religion, which is essentially a belief in something bigger than yourself.

Oxytocin is a neuropeptide in the brain, and a hormone in the blood, that performs a diverse variety of functions. Here, however, we'll focus on the functions that have the most significant implications for human psychology. Now let me explain why you might want to add more oxytocin to your daily Angel's cocktail. Oxytocin is amazing – actually it's better than amazing! It's the substance that contributes to your feeling of presence, completeness and – in the right contexts – trust, compassion, connectedness and generosity.

Imagine walking up to a stranger in the street and giving them a hug. Will this elevate their oxytocin levels and make them more trusting, compassionate, connected and generous towards you? Hardly. But if you give a friend a comforting warm hug, they are more likely to feel trusting, compassionate, connected and generous. This means, then, that oxytocin is context-dependent, and usually needs to be triggered gradually between people. Unfortunately, like all substances, there is also a dark side to oxytocin, which I will return to. For now, let's take a deep dive into the light side of oxytocin, and talk about how you can dose yourself with it every day, as often as you like.

I want you to read those words one more time: presence, completeness, compassion, connectedness, generosity, trust. Pause here for a moment. Don't read on yet. Take those words in, and consider the enormous impact they have on your life and your relationships.

Let's visit Duncan again – our friend from the late Stone Age. It's Friday, about 25,000 years ago, and it's a day he will never forget. As usual, Duncan is inside his humble hut made from mammoth tusks, tree branches and clay. He's lying inside, listening to the patter of the rain outside and admiring the basket of red wild apples that he gathered over the last week. In his peaceful satisfaction, he realizes that he must be hallucinating again, because he has a strong sense that somebody is standing outside the hut, knocking on his mammoth tusks and clearing their throat. He turns to gaze at his straw wall and thinks to himself that he's had to become accustomed to hallucinations after some unfortunate experiences as a result of sampling a large variety of forest mushrooms. However, this hallucination seems different: it carries on, most persistently, without changing at all. Suddenly he freezes – surely this can't really be happening? There's no way! He stays in bed, immobile, unable to decide if what he's feeling is panic or bliss. It's been so long since he came across somebody of his own kind that he hardly even remembers what he looks like. Another knock. Duncan climbs off his straw bed and walks over to the doorway, where he comes across an exhausted, soaked and worn-out woman of his own kind. She has the most beautiful face he has ever seen.

If Duncan's brain hadn't been able to produce oxytocin, he probably would have just shut the door in her face and gone back to bed. But thanks to oxytocin and other substances, Duncan is struck by empathy for this stranger, who's in quite a state, and immediately ushers her into his hut and offers her a seat by his crackling fire.

The days go by, and they talk over cups of blueberry tea and apple pie. Her name is Grace, and she explains that she got lost several months ago and never found her way back to her own tribe. The more they learn about one another, the more oxytocin they produce, and the tighter their bond grows. They start making physical contact with one another, which triggers even greater releases of oxytocin, until, one day, they fall passionately in love, which soon leads to sexual interactions that boost their oxytocin even more. Nine months later, your ancestors Duncan and Grace become parents when their two beautiful children, Elsie and Ivor, come into the world. The oxytocin that connects them all constitutes an unbreakable bond. They are a family now, and they respect, love and listen to each other. The oxytocin also bonds them to their habitat, the place where they live. It makes them love that particular place, and all the memories they've made there.

Back to Reality

Have you ever noticed that misunderstandings, friction and arguments all seem to happen more frequently in your relationships when the oxytocin runs low? This is what happens when we don't communicate, touch or find time for one another. The opposite of this is what happens when the people in a relationship *do* touch, communicate and find time for each other. There's a funny and ancient piece of advice on this theme: never make an important decision before sex – or after sex! In a study carried out by Andrea L. Meltzer of Florida State University it was discovered that both parties experienced a significant improvement in their relationship after sex, which lasted for up to forty-eight hours. This, then, is a scientifically established reason for you to engage in sexual activity at least every forty-eight hours! During sex, vast quantities of oxytocin and other substances are released in the brain. A similar effect, though not as strong, happens during more subtle physical interactions, like long hugs, kisses, massage, touch, eye contact and even kind gestures and active listening. You could hardly go wrong if you stopped reading here, and just made a point of including those eight ingredients in your relationship. As you've no doubt noticed on countless occasions, the positive effects of a good relationship tend to impact most areas of your life. But there is a lot more for you to learn and do here, of course, so keep reading.

When people ask me 'how can I be a good friend?', 'how can I become popular?' or 'how can I be the kind of person others want to spend time with?', my answer is simple: make yourself the best listener you can possibly be and learn to take an interest in other people. In my experience, the most popular individuals in people's lives, the ones who deliver the most oxytocin, are the active listeners, the individuals who care and show consideration. We don't forget them. On the contrary, we care about them, and we show them respect. If you were to pause here, and just think about your friends, I'm sure you'd be able to name and list the people in your life who genuinely care when you share something about yourself, whether it's something positive or negative. And, in all likelihood, thinking of these people will bring a smile to your face.

Apart from spending lots of time with our loved ones, we spend a great deal of time in our workplaces. Oxytocin plays a huge role there too, and can even have an impact on the success of the business. In a culture where co-workers care about each other, help each other and share bonds of loyalty, oxytocin and profits will both be in abundant supply.

Now that we understand the psychological impact of oxytocin on our well-being, the time has come to slip into our bartender's braces again and learn how to produce more oxytocin in ourselves and in others as we go about our daily lives. We'll also reflect on how you already use it in your own life today, and how you might begin to if you don't.

Tool 1: Awe

Let's begin with awe, the emotion we discussed in the introduction to this chapter. Awe is an emotional response to becoming aware of the existence of something larger than ourselves, something that we find difficult to comprehend. Awe could, for example, be triggered by the powerful experiences of art and music, or, more commonly, nature. It can also be triggered by powerful collective experiences, like during concerts or large political rallies. But let's start our exploration in the forest. Imagine a deciduous forest, with towering oaks, elms and maples, where the first autumn leaves have just begun to cover the ground. A curious woodpecker is swooping between the trees. In a study by Virginia E. Sturm of Berkeley University in California, participants were asked to spend fifteen minutes each day walking through a forest much like the one in our example. They were supposed to take these daily walks through the woods for eight weeks, and take selfies at specific times during their walks. One group also received an instruction handout that included the following: *During your walk, try to approach what you see with fresh eyes, imagining that you're seeing it for the first time. Take a moment in each walk to take in the vastness of things, for example in looking at a panoramic view or up close at the detail of a leaf or flower.* The other group were given no further instruction, and were simply told to walk and take pictures of themselves. Then both groups were asked to evaluate each walk in a survey, and the group that was instructed to experience awe reported a gradually improving capacity to do so, and an increasing sense of reverence after each walk. Their self-evaluations also showed a rise in prosocial emotions, such as compassion and gratitude, in comparison with the control group who just went walking.

What fascinates me most about this study is that the participants of the awe walk group began to take their selfies in a new way. Two aspects of their photos changed. The first was that, as the weeks went by, their faces and bodies started to occupy less of the image space. The second change was that they were displaying an increasing number of genuine smiles. Virginia E. Sturm commented: 'One of the key features of awe is that it promotes what we call "small self", a healthy sense of proportion between your own self and the bigger picture of the world around you.' It was evident that the reflections and thoughts of the participants in the awe walk group had transitioned from being self-centred and problem-oriented to being more holistic and appreciative.

So how can you use awe to add an Angel's cocktail of oxytocin to your everyday life? By making yourself aware of the grandness that exists in small things. Practise indulging your sense of astonishment over how a stone came into being, how birds can fly, how each autumn leaf falls in its very own way and how every snowflake is unique. Be aware, though, that we tend to focus on visual impressions, because sight is our dominant sense. Don't forget to also experience smells, sounds, physical sensations and your own thoughts about all the wondrous, unique phenomena that surround us.

While we're at it, I'd also like to share another fascinating study of awe, which was led by Yann Auxéméry. Seventy-two military veterans and fifty-two troubled young adults were given an opportunity to go white-water rafting and encouraged to experience awe during the excursion. The results were compared with groups who went rafting but received no instructions specifically mentioning awe. The awe group reported a 29 per cent reduction in symptoms of PTSD, a 21 per cent reduction of stress, a 10 per cent improvement in social relationships, a 9 per cent better life satisfaction and 8 per cent better happiness. Those are some truly remarkable numbers, especially when you consider that they all came down to one single factor: deliberately pausing and attempting to experience awe.

It's important to mention here that in studies where participants were asked to experience awe at things created by humans, such as architecture, the effects were generally much weaker.

Tool 2: Empathy

Here's an excellent tip for how you can add an immediate boost of oxytocin to your Angel's cocktail: when you get home to your family after a hectic day of meetings, frantic work activity and heated discussions, pause for a moment in your car or outside your front door. Pick up your smartphone and take a look at a clip that triggers your empathy, like cute kittens, people helping each other or someone you love. A couple of minutes will do it. Then go inside. The difference this can make is enormous. If you simply barge in, drunk on a Devil's cocktail mixed from strong doses of cortisol and fast dopamine, you might not even register their attempts to make eye contact, or truly feel their embraces and hear what they say to you. But now, thanks to a strategic dose of oxytocin, you'll be able to genuinely see, feel and hear them. They will notice the difference too. People say that time is the most valuable currency in the world, but I'd like to claim that presence is the true gold standard.

This tip can be just as useful to you in your professional life, especially if you happen to be a manager or salesperson. A boost of oxytocin can make quite a difference in stressful situations like meetings, presentations and negotiations. You might recognize this scenario: you've prepared fully and invested twelve hours of work into your slideshow. Your belt is adjusted just so, your shoes are shined and you feel ready to make a good impression. However, the moment you step on the stage, you find yourself tongue-tied and your brain slows to a halt. You can't remember a word of the script that you've practised to perfection! You make your way through the presentation, sweating profusely, and end up leaving the stage without the faintest clue as to what you actually ended up saying. What happened here? The answer is that you overdosed on cortisol and adrenaline, and that your brain suddenly decided that your audience was a hostile group of sabretooth tigers. If you had known that you just needed to give your brain a shot of oxytocin before stepping on the stage, you could have better controlled the situation and delivered a stronger performance. Oxytocin, you see, has the wonderful benefits of reducing both your cortisol levels and your blood pressure.

In my role as a lecturer, I have been on thousands of stages. I've also analysed thousands of other speakers and concluded that the mistake that so many make is to spend the final few minutes before the speech begins going over the introduction or script, or thinking about questions that might come up. All this produces more stress than anybody needs. My recommendation, instead, is to spend those last ten minutes entering a desired mental state. I usually look at a picture of my daughter when she had just turned seven, in which she's running across a meadow and flashing a smile that could melt the heart of a marble statue. After that, I step on the stage in a state far more conducive to being present, both for myself and for my audience. You'll also notice that your ability to give and remember your presentation will be vastly improved if you have some oxytocin in your body, rather than being flushed with cortisol and stress. High stress levels tend to limit our access to our short-term memories. I've gone through this process so many times now that just thinking of that picture produces a misty film over my eyes and wraps me up in a fluffy blanket of empathy.

Tool 3: Touch

The first physical encounter between two humans isn't too different from a peacock flamboyantly showing off its feathers to attract a mate. While our displays tend to be clumsier and less efficient, they're all the more entertaining for that. When we meet a stranger for the first time, we maintain our distance, perhaps giving them a nod or – if we're feeling bold – a long handshake with arm fully extended. Assuming both of us realize that there is mutual benefit to be made, our next encounter might involve a softer handshake, this time without the classic forward lean. The dance escalates, and by the time meeting number three arrives, one of us might have found the courage to touch the other's shoulder or arm – perhaps we might sit a little closer during lunch. A few weeks later, we've moved on to hugging as a greeting, and presto! Thanks to this systematic 'dance of touch', we'll have become closer, established mutual trust and learned to work better together. This dance is, of course, culturally dependent, but wherever you go the main ingredient will be gradual physical closeness and care.

There's no need at all for any red wine and romantic subtexts here – this is a process, or dance, that most people go through when they get to know each other in all kinds of relationships. This isn't too strange really, when you consider that oxytocin is secreted whenever somebody touches us, and that this is what we're subconsciously striving for. Assaulting a random stranger by giving them a twenty-second hug followed by intense eye contact is actually antisocial, as behaviour goes, but the very same behaviour tends to be expected and appreciated between close friends.

It's perhaps not too strange then that some people felt more affected than others by the isolation that we all went through during the peak of the Covid-19 pandemic. This was a time in our lives when twelve-packs of cans of oxytocin would have flown off the shelves if they were available for purchase. We collectively experienced a degree of isolation that was perhaps unprecedented in modern times. Studies have also shown that this didn't exactly do wonders for our mental health; the lack of human contact led to a rise in mental problems like anxiety and depression.

But that's not all. Another study into the importance of oxytocin was conducted by Sheldon Cohen from Carnegie Mellon University in Pittsburgh. If somebody called you one day to ask you if you'd let them infect you with a common cold virus as part of a study, you would probably respond with caution and scepticism. Nonetheless, the team managed to recruit 406 participants. The participants were given self-assessment surveys for two weeks to track the number of conflicts they experienced in their relationships, and how many hugs they received. After this, all 406 were exposed to the virus. Astonishingly – or perhaps not so astonishingly – the subjects who had received a lot of hugs were less prone to infection, and those who were infected experienced less severe symptoms, while the immune systems of those who received fewer hugs and experienced more conflict had a much harder time. A study on coyotes had similar results, which suggested that a lack of oxytocin caused by isolation could actually cause cell death.

To positively influence your own Angel's cocktail with touch, you should simply strive to be close to somebody, spend time with friends, invite closeness in others, hug people or hold hands. Bear in mind that you can also achieve the same effects by interacting with animals. Most studies into this have used dogs, but it's probable that we would get the same results if we were to study the effects of other animals that we think of as our 'best friends'. If you lack opportunities for closeness, from both humans and animals, you can also achieve the sensation of being touched by activating sensory nerves through the application of light to moderate static pressure on your skin. One way of doing this is to sleep with a weighted blanket, according to research conducted by Kerstin Uvnäs Moberg. While we're on the topic of blankets – you know that incredibly cosy feeling that you get when you're cold and you climb into a warm bed, freshly made with crisp, clean bedclothes? Even though no study I'm aware of has shown that this produces oxytocin specifically, the feeling it gives me seems very similar to my experience of oxytocin in other situations. One study that might lend credence to this theory, however, was conducted by Leo Pruimboom and Daniel Reheis, who managed to show that oxytocin is released in situations where we experience heat, like when we take hot showers. So if we add one and one together, and establish that the blanket stimulates sensory nerves in the skin, while retaining your own bodily heat, it does seem rather plausible that the cosy feeling I described above is fuelled at least in part by oxytocin.

Tool 4: Generosity

Being generous is an absolute favourite approach of mine when I need to boost the oxytocin content in my Angel's cocktail. The brilliant thing about plain old kindness is that it can bring about a kind of self-reinforcing feedback that motivates us to be even more generous in future. In a study by Jorge A. Barraza and Paul J. Zak, a group of participants were shown emotionally neutral video clips, while another group were shown empathy-triggering videos, like people going through a crisis or acting considerately to each other. The participants in the empathy-engendering group experienced an oxytocin boost of about 47 per cent compared to the baseline. When I think back on my own career, I've met salespeople who have told me quite bluntly 'you share too much content; there's no way to pitch and sell you.' I suspect that it's actually the other way round, and that this was what laid the foundation for my success as a speaker. Always sharing for the point of sharing, and never expecting anything in return is a powerful strategy.

Earlier in my life, I co-owned a fishing-tackle shop with a friend of mine. I loved fishing, and so I thought to myself,

Why not open a fishing-tackle shop? It also made a great change from lecturing. Like many other fishing shops, we used to go to fishing conventions, which were all rather unique experiences. The one I'm thinking of here was particularly unusual. It happened in northern Sweden, a place of magical beauty. I was standing in our booth on the first day when a man came by to check out our fishing equipment. While we spoke, I asked him if he knew of any good fishing spots nearby that I might take my team to that evening. He brightened up like the sun! He described the way to his favourite spot most passionately, but as I couldn't make sense of his directions, he drew me a map. When it was finally five o'clock, and time to close up for the day, he returned and said, 'You know what? I'll show you instead – I realize now that the map I made is rather messy.' So we drove after him for fifteen miles or so – it was completely out of his way! – and when we arrived, he told us, 'Since you don't have a boat, you can use mine. The key is right over there. Just return it to the same spot when you're done.' He was bright and cheerful, and so were we! But it didn't end there. On the last day of the fair, he came back to us, and said, 'Next time you visit, you can stay in my cabin. I don't use it during the convention anyway. Oh, and you can have it free of charge!' I had to ask him why he was being so kind to us. 'I'm kind to everybody; it makes them and me both feel great – it's like the elixir of life,' he said, laughing.

This memory of him became etched in my mind, and I began to see what he meant about generosity being an elixir of life. One ingredient of this magic potion is definitely oxytocin, although dopamine clearly plays a part too.

The oxytocin levels in our bodies, you see, have been shown to rise significantly when we help other humans, which in turn reduces our stress levels and improves our health. Interestingly enough our oxytocin levels increase naturally as we age, which generally means that the older we get, the more helpful we become.

Tool 5: Eye Contact

If an academic named Arthur Aron ever asks you to spend ten minutes posing a series of intimate questions to a stranger, and then spend four minutes making eye contact with them, you might find what comes next easier to deal with if you happen to be single. It turned out, you see, that this study caused some of its participants to discover 'emotions of love' for one another – one couple even got married six months after participating.

Perhaps it's not that remarkable that eye contact between humans can trigger an oxytocin release, and maybe we could guess that interacting with animals would have the same results, but did you know that it also seems to work through video? According to a study conducted by Tampere University in Finland, eye contact through video can bring about similar psychological effects as actual encounters in physical space, but only if the video connection is a live one. During the Covid-19 pandemic, I gave hundreds of digital lectures to people all over the world on how to lecture, present and conduct meetings in the digital space. I often used the participants' cameras to provide examples, and would make comments like: 'I see that today we have twelve nose-hair examination angles, eight forehead projections, five earwax analyses and two people who actually gave it some thought.' What I was referring to, of course, was how the participants had angled their webcams. On average, only two members of each group would receive a pass. What did they do differently from the rest? They positioned their cameras in line with their eyes, and positioned a light source to give their faces a warm glow. They looked straight into the camera, and they looked alive. After this, I would ask everyone to spend ten minutes adjusting their camera set-ups. The change it brought about was astonishing! It made such an incredible difference for people to be able to look one another in the eye. Some of them, however, felt disappointed. 'So you mean we've spent almost eighteen months getting it completely wrong, and weakening our sense of connectedness?' It's quite a fail, I guess, if you look at it that way.

I'm often asked if there's a pill you can take to give yourself an oxytocin boost. And, in truth, one of the primary substances released from recreational drugs like MDMA or ecstasy is oxytocin, but this is a shortcut that's hardly sustainable, and which can be harmful, of course.

Despite the existence of artificial oxytocin sources, I believe that it's always better to learn to use the power of our own brains instead. The interesting thing here is that a whole list of long-term effects, including lowered blood pressure, lowered cortisol levels, improved stress tolerance, pain relief, quicker healing, improved ability to read facial expressions and detect intonation in voices and countless other prosocial effects like wanting to spend more time with other people, can often be achieved by producing oxytocin through non-medical means. These include having a strong network of people around you, and spending time with the people you like.

Tool 6: Soothing Music

Have you ever given any thought to why you sometimes listen to soothing music? There are probably lots of reasons, but your body might be smart enough to realize that it needs it. According to a study by Ulrica Nilsson of the Karolinska Institute, something as simple as listening to calm music for half an hour can boost oxytocin levels in post-operation patients and thus speed up their recuperation. In other words, you can deliberately choose to listen to soothing music whenever you want to reduce your stress and improve your recovery. That's self-leadership in action for you.

If you want to take it a step further and derive even more oxytocin from music, you can always sing! You see, singing boosts your oxytocin levels, and this is true whether you happen to be a rank amateur or a professional singer, according to a Swedish study carried out by Christina Grape and her team at Uppsala University. An interesting discovery they made was that when both groups (amateurs and professionals) were asked to self-assess their well-being after singing, the amateurs reported feeling improved happiness and elation, while the professionals didn't, though both groups did report feeling more focused and relaxed. The professional singers put a lot of emphasis on their performance, which caused them to secrete more cortisol, while the amateurs focused on just expressing themselves, and thus reduced their cortisol levels instead. This small difference in attitude can make a huge difference – your mindset can alter the effects of oxytocin and your cortisol levels! If I step on stage to give a speech with a mindset that's focused on my upcoming performance, my experience will be completely different to if I adopt a mindset that emphasizes having fun. In my experience, when you choose to focus on enjoying yourself, a good performance will follow almost automatically. However, if you focus on your performance, you're unlikely to gain enjoyment and fun as side effects. Instead, the side effects are more likely to be a combination of performance anxiety and stress. So, my friend, here is a little bonus tip for you: practise enjoying yourself and having fun in every way you can – as this will automatically elevate how you perform.

Tool 7: Hot and Cold Exposure

It may seem a little paradoxical that oxytocin is released both when we're exposed to heat and when we're exposed to cold, but as you're about to learn, it actually makes sense. First of all, oxytocin is triggered by heat, like when we take a warm bath, sit in a sauna or get into a warm car when it's windy and below freezing outside. All these situations have one thing in common: they relieve and relax us. That's precisely what we need after any amount of time in a cold-water bath or a hot sauna. Oxytocin, you see, has been shown to be released during stress, and what could possibly be more stressful to the body than an icy bath or a sauna? Our adrenaline and noradrenaline will spike, our body's stress responses will grow intense and oxytocin will be released to wind everything down.

Tool 8: Gratitude

Gratitude is an emotion that has near-magical powers. It can improve well-being, reduce stress and aid recovery from certain injuries and afflictions. Let's begin by examining gratitude in three different scenarios. We're going to follow three individuals who are checking into the same hotel.

The first person has an ungrateful outlook on life and constantly looks for flaws in everything around her. When she arrives at the hotel, she's annoyed at having to wait ten minutes for an electric car charger. Once that's been arranged and her car is charging, she slams her shoulder into the revolving door because it's moving so slowly. When she arrives at the reception, the queue is ten minutes long, again, and she spends all this time thinking about how idiotic the hotel's layout is, how the children nearby are being too loud and how much her shoulder hurts. She finally receives her key, but since the lift is out of order, she has to take the stairs. She hisses to herself, 'Is this what I'm paying for?'

The second person embodies the Buddhist philosophy of maintaining a neutral emotional state. Like the first individual, she has to wait for a car charger, she also bumps into the slowly revolving door, she stands in line and she has to climb two staircases. However, she does all this without evaluating it as negative or positive. She opens the door to her room, and never gives any of it another thought. She just accepts things as they are, and this attitude makes her feel great.

The third and final person arrives at the hotel and gives off a delighted little shout. 'Yay! They have electric car chargers! Lucky me!' While waiting for her car to charge, she relishes the thought of having a fully charged car ready to go for the next stage of her journey tomorrow. On the way into the hotel, she bumps her shoulder on the slowly revolving door but simply laughs, grateful for the reminder that she shouldn't rush about all the time. Inside the hotel, she finds the most gorgeous foyer, enjoys the scents that are wafting over from the restaurant, and admires the artworks, the architecture, the colours and the furniture. 'Sorry, sorry, welcome! Can I help you check in, please?' She hasn't even noticed that her ten minutes of standing in line are up. She gratefully accepts the key and walks over to the lift, which turns out to be out of order. But this only reminds her of a book she read that explained how people are too lazy in general, and always choose the escalator, so she just laughs, and says to herself, 'That's perfect, now I'll get some staircase exercise in today!' Once this person arrives in her room, she will have downed an entire Angel's cocktail, thanks to her oxytocin-rich emotions of appreciation, gratitude, happiness and pleasure.

Most findings would suggest that your life will be improved if you can train your mind to respond to different situations like individuals two or three. The Buddhist mindset of accepting things the way they are, and not considering them good or bad, can be fantastic! It's particularly useful in situations where you're likely to experience quick transitions between feelings of success and failure. An example of this could be social media. If you post something that receives a poor response, this can affect you negatively, while it can give your mood an incredible boost to post something that receives a good response. However, being too strongly impacted by other people's reactions in this way can end up feeling like an unpleasant emotional rollercoaster ride, and the Buddhist mindset can be a great way of dealing with this. Alternatively we could emulate person three: rather than focusing on other people's reactions, we can emphasize the fun we had taking the photo. This will help distance us from the negative emotions we might experience as a result of direct or indirect criticism from others.

But what about the first individual? Are there no benefits at all to behaving that way? Well, I reckon you'll be old and grey before you find a single scientific study that suggests that repeated negative behaviour and chronic ingratitude provide any kind of health benefits. Neutrality, positivity or some combination of the two will help you make better decisions, feel better, enjoy better relationships, suffer less illness, live longer and other stuff that matters in life.

During my years of struggling with depressive thoughts, gratitude was something I distinctly lacked. I was ungrateful

basically – always looking for (and finding) flaws in everything. It seems obvious to me now that this played a huge
part in my feeling the way I did. I was spewing up negative
thoughts every day, and this was putting me in a state of
constant stress, which in turn kept my serotonin levels low
and made my body more susceptible to inflammation. What
about oxytocin? I didn't see much of that, to be honest; my
only quantitive source of oxytocin was from physical closeness with my wife – a situation that made me entirely
dependent on another person for my oxytocin supply.
I didn't know any better, of course, but that kind of depend-
ence is never much fun for either party in a romantic
relationship. It's supposed to be mutual and unconditional,
after all. In other words, I wasn't exactly making things any
easier for myself.

My journey was a long one, but eventually I began to
practise experiencing gratitude. I did this in part through
meditations in which I focused on being grateful for people,
events, things, myself and my own successes. I kept a journal and wrote an entry daily, making a point of including
three things I was grateful for on that particular day. After
a while, I stopped writing and started doing it when I lay
in bed, just thinking about those three things. This proved
to be just as effective, and today, seven years later, I still
perform this gratitude exercise almost every morning and
evening. I used to have to put in an incredible amount of
effort to turn my ungrateful, negative thoughts into grateful, positive ones – and this is a skill I still need to practise
today. My life now is full of gratitude, compared to the
way it was, but in stressful situations my old feelings of

ingratitude tend to re-emerge, and I find myself having to actively force them into submission, and I replace them with this question: what do I feel grateful for?

'Dark' Oxytocin

Life isn't all peaches and cream, you know. Like most things, oxytocin has downsides, and most of us have experienced these in some way or other, although usually without being consciously aware of them. It's time we took a look at how oxytocin can also be an ingredient in a Devil's cocktail. I'd like to introduce you to a fictional business; let's call it Cruel-T Inc. Like many other companies, it has a product development team and a sales team. Unfortunately both these teams have subconsciously chosen to use dark oxytocin to establish a sense of belonging within their respective team members. The salespeople talk about the product development team behind their backs, calling them lazy slobs and 'emotionless engineers'. Their coffee breaks revolve around discussing how awful certain members of the product development team are, and there are rumours circulating about how they all earn far more money than they have any right to. It doesn't matter if any of this is true or not, as long as it serves to put them down. The product development team naturally behaves the same way back. Is this going to work? Yes, it's going to work. Businesses today work just fine. It's my opinion, based on all the companies I've visited and worked for, that this kind of dark oxytocin is a far more common binding agent within businesses than light oxytocin. And, yeah, it works! But when you think about it, 'it works' is a pretty low standard. People in organizations could be feeling so much better and achieving so much more.

To be absolutely clear, oxytocin doesn't literally have different shades or colours in your body. My use of 'dark' and 'light' here is metaphorical; it's a way for me to make it clear to you that oxytocin has two sides, and while they are often opposing, each can produce similar results. Oxytocin is thought to be a factor contributing to those who hold radical beliefs. Our desire to belong to a group is so powerful that it can even overcome our own moral and ethical convictions. Belonging to a group is often more important than most other things in life!

Here's an interesting thought experiment you can try: the next time you experience a setback or friction between yourself and a close friend, perhaps even your partner, pay attention to how you go about 'patching it up'. It's incredibly common for people in this situation to suddenly choose to resort to gossiping about how other couples or friends are in even worse relationships or experiencing even worse emotions. Putting other people down to elevate yourself, as an attempt to repair the damage done by a conflict, is a good example of how 'dark' oxytocin is often used. Instead, you should practise repairing your relationships through acts of consideration, listening, acceptance and respect. If you're a manager or leader, you should be encouraging your team members to create a sense of belonging within their teams through 'light' oxytocin, rather than 'dark' oxytocin.

So what is light oxytocin? It's all the things we've discussed in this chapter. It's when you form bonds with others by listening attentively to them, showing vulnerability, behaving generously, showing gratitude, inviting participation and being kind. If you're a manager or leader in your professional role, you'd do well to avoid segregating activities like competitions between departments. It's usually a better idea to encourage inter-department collaborations, so that people get to know each other during activities and while performing work tasks.

One day, I received a phone call from a woman who explained to me the challenges she was facing in her HR role stemming from a huge dysfunction that existed within the company's management team. The company was a big one, one of the major listed companies in Sweden, and she felt that a large part of the explanation for their recent lack of success was how friction and differences of opinion were being handled within the management team. So she asked me, 'You've spent a lot of time coaching people – what would your advice be?' I asked her some follow-up questions, and then gave her a promise. 'Give me two hours, and I reckon I can fix it!' She laughed. 'You can't imagine how hard we've tried! What good is two hours going to be?' I described my oxytocin-based approach, and she almost immediately agreed. Once I arrived, I instilled a sense of security in the management team. I started out slow, and then asked them all to share a setback in their lives that had had a big impact on them. They went on doing this, in varied forms, for two hours. After this two-hour session, their faces were streaked with tears

and make-up, and they were hugging each other and viewing each other in a different light than they had before.
Two hours of this created a stronger sense of connectedness than countless efforts over the past few years,
which had ultimately achieved nothing but the boosting
of dark oxytocin.

It's incredibly important not to rush these kinds of
things. Oxytocin takes time, and you have to dial up the
intensity slowly. You can't form a connection by simply
running up to a stranger in the street, hugging them and
gazing deeply into their eyes while asking them ten intimate questions. Dark oxytocin functions similarly. Groups
of bullies are formed gradually, through a succession of
subtle jabs and acts of dominance, which gradually intensify through actions that serve to strengthen the group by
belittling some other group or person. Try to make yourself aware of any such tendencies in your own behaviour,
or the behaviour of others. If you can catch dark oxytocin
out in time, you might be able to stop it from spreading
like a virus.

I've tried, for a very long time, to follow the maxim of
never speaking ill of others behind their backs. Sometimes,
when things get turbulent between me and a friend, say,
I will feel the instinctive urge to say something unpleasant
about somebody else, but I'm at the point now when I can
usually stop myself. I view this behaviour as a warning
sign – if somebody speaks ill of somebody else to me, it
seems very likely that they might also be doing the same of
me to others. It's far better to talk directly to the person in
question instead.

Tool 9: Your Thoughts

I'd like to close this chapter by discussing storytelling and its connections to oxytocin and emotions in general. You could think of your life as a story, a narrative complete with characters, setbacks and successes. It's very likely that your brain is full of hundreds of thousands of little stories that you repeat to yourself from time to time. Every encounter, every event you remember, is a story. When we listen to a story about a character we can relate to, oxytocin is released. When we listen to a story that causes stress in us, cortisol is released. The storytelling technique can play just as big a part in generating emotion as the actual contents of the story. Memory can cause the events to magnify significantly, as you repeat them countless times when recalling them. If you choose to repeat your past experiences of gratitude, happiness and reverence, rather than your experiences of the opposite emotions, you'll be boosting your Angel's cocktail rather than your Devil's cocktail. So this is the recipe: learn to observe your thoughts, make yourself aware of the narratives your brain is trying to get you to think about, reflect on whether the stories involved make you feel better or not, and then proceed to make any changes you deem necessary. Start right away and stick with it by stubbornly steamrollering any negative narratives that pop up. It can take months for your brain to begin automatically telling you positive stories about yourself and your current and past experiences, but it's worth the time and effort.

How can you get better at observing automatic thoughts? I have three suggestions:

1. Focus meditation is an excellent technique for adding distance between the thoughts you're thinking and your decision whether to carry on thinking them.

2. Mindfulness is focusing on whatever you're currently doing. Any time you catch yourself not being mindful, that's actually proof that you're being mindful! Think of catching your mind out when it drifts as a success, rather than a defeat.

3. Speak to yourself in the third person, engaging in a dialogue with yourself, saying something like: 'There you are, having a read. Are you well, is everything good?' Awareness of your own thoughts can be achieved quite quickly, but no matter how long it takes, it's worth doing. Once you possess this ability, you'll have unlocked the door to being in full control of your thoughts. Try it out by setting this book aside for a moment, and asking yourself some questions in the third person.

I've been practising observing my own thoughts for some time now, almost seven years, which means that I can hear almost everything that passes through my brain – every word, every character and narrative it chooses to make me think about. I'm rarely surprised by the things my brain chooses either. Most of its choices are fairly predictable, but it does occasionally produce a thought

I wasn't expecting. When this happens, I spend a moment trying to figure out where this idea might have come from: was it a newspaper article I read, a film I saw, somebody who said something to me or a scent that triggered something within me? I always figure it out eventually, and it's a lot of fun to do! It's like mental detective work! So you can imagine my surprise when one day, my brain, seemingly out of nowhere, decided to produce a whole load of depressive thoughts, emotions, memories and stories. I was shocked, and I told my wife, 'It's so strange that this is happening to me. I have no idea why – I've tried to figure it out, taken notes, made a mind map and studied all the possible causes, but I still have no clue . . .' It went on like this until, two days later, after reading countless studies, I learned something that would prove absolutely decisive for me, a fact concerning the relationship between serotonin and inflammation. We'll go over that in the next chapter. Before we move on, though, I've saved the best of all the oxytocin tools for last.

Tool 10: Ho'oponopono

Out of the hundreds of tools I teach, I hold no doubt at all that this is the most powerful of all. *Ho'oponopono* is a Hawaiian practice that aims to neutralize an individual's guilt and debts to other people. It involves uttering the following four incredible phrases: *I love you, I am sorry, please forgive me, thank you.*

I believe in taking action, so let's try this out right away.

It's quite important that you learn the phrases by heart first, so you can utter them to yourself without thinking about it. Once that's done, sit down comfortably, close your eyes and speak the phrases to yourself in your mind, to those people who have had a positive or negative impact on your life. You can finish by directing it at yourself too. The power of this tool is enormous, and around half of those who try it find themselves crying tears of gratitude. Feel free to put some soothing music on in the background too. This will make your oxytocin stacking even more powerful. You might as well get some tissues ready as well – you may need them. Enjoy!

I once had a participant in one of my classes who told me about how his boss had behaved terribly to him during his first year of work, and how despite receiving some vindication in the form of a half-hearted apology, he still had to face his boss every day at work. Each time he felt it like a stab to the chest. The pain wouldn't go away, and no matter what he did, it just kept getting more and more intense, until he heard me describe *Ho'oponopono* on a podcast. He was determined to make a change, and decided to repeat those phrases to himself in his mind every time he ran into his boss, which was several times a day. Three weeks later, he noticed how his pain and negative emotions seemed to have somehow melted away effortlessly, and a month later he was able to encounter his boss without any negative emotions at all. This story is just one of countless others like it that I've been told over the years by participants who have applied *Ho'oponopono* in their lives.

Oxytocin – A Summary

No Angel's cocktail would be complete without oxytocin. It's oxytocin that allows you to enjoy human closeness, security, connectedness and belonging. Oxytocin makes you human, and oxytocin heals you. You should help set the stage for it every morning, and throughout every day, by seeking out opportunities to experience awe and wonder, and maintaining a deliberately grateful mindset. Produce oxytocin by interacting socially, opening yourself to others, sharing, conversing, caring about others and helping them. Every moment that includes closeness and empathy is a particularly important one. Whether you're coming back home to your family, preparing for a date or heading into a performance appraisal, you should add some extra oxytocin to your Angel's cocktail, perhaps by performing *Ho'oponopono* or by looking at pictures in your smartphone that are guaranteed to trigger feelings of empathy and compassion.

Serotonin

Social Status, Contentment and Mood

I love serotonin! The feelings of contentedness, stability and not having to be constantly on the hunt for something provide me with a great basic sense of happiness. Serotonin is probably the most difficult to grasp of the substances we'll discuss in this book, but if you'll just bear with me, I'll make sure to get you through this chapter without any trouble. To establish a clear context for our discussion of serotonin, I'd like us to go back in time again. We're about to check in with our Stone Age friends Duncan and Grace and explore some of the connections between serotonin and social status.

Social Status

It's 25,000 years ago. Duncan and Grace are the informal leaders of their tribe, and all is well in their world. Their lives are generally harmonious and free from stress. They are both situated at the top of the social order, which means that they probably have the highest serotonin levels in their tribe. They have everything they need: access to food, a partner and somewhere to live. Naturally they also wear the best-quality furs of anyone in the tribe and have the most beautifully decorated hiking sticks. That is until one day when everything changes. Duncan and Grace spot a large group of individuals approaching from a distance. They run back to the village, as fast as they can, to warn everyone else. Everybody is soon on their feet, ready to greet the strangers. Will they prove to be friendly or hostile? The strangers seem good-natured enough, but they're obviously more technologically advanced than Duncan and Grace's tribe. Their behaviour is more sophisticated, and they wear furs you could only dream of – and let's not even mention their hiking sticks! The inhabitants soon flock to these new individuals, who seem to be claiming more and more space in the group. Duncan and Grace begin to feel that their social status is being threatened, and that their reliable access to food, a partner and somewhere to live is endangered along with it. Their stress increases significantly. The harmonious feelings that their serotonin used to produce are gone, and have been replaced by anxiety. Grace becomes very frustrated, and heads into the woods for a walk to calm herself down. But it doesn't help. Enraged, she hurls a piece of flint at a larger rock, which produces a spark! Her motivation spikes as she experiences a dopamine rush – what was that? She tries it again, and again, until she realizes that she can reliably make fire with these two rocks. Grace runs back to the village to demonstrate her discovery. Nobody in the community can believe their eyes. Fire from rocks? What an amazing invention! Duncan and Grace become heroes once more and reclaim their places as the leaders of the tribe. Their serotonin levels go back up, and their harmonious feelings return, as they are once more at the top of the social order with guaranteed access to food, a partner and somewhere to live.

Back to Reality

Serotonin has been shown to be tightly linked to social status. The individuals who enjoy the highest status also have the highest levels of serotonin. These people tend to be the most harmonious, the least stressed and the healthiest, because of their feeling that they have access to everything they need and aren't under threat. The moment their social status, or perceived social status, is threatened, this will affect their serotonin, and if stress should arise as a result, this can, in turn, provoke aggression. Those who believe they occupy (or actually do occupy) the lowest rungs of the social hierarchy will tend to have the lowest serotonin levels, and suffer frequent stress and poor health as a result. In terms of the world of Duncan and Grace that we just visited, the least privileged members of the tribe will never know if the rabbit they just caught is going to end up being theirs or be taken by somebody higher up in the pecking order.

We share our biological responses to social status with most mammals, but humans are set apart in two important ways. First of all, we exist in multiple simultaneous social orders, which means that our social status can change several times during a single day. Your day might begin with being told off by your boss in the coffee room at the office. Everybody looks at you in silence, and you wander back to your workstation feeling rather downtrodden. Your social status has taken a blow, and your serotonin has dropped along with it. Six hours later, however, you're at the local bowling alley, where you happen to be something of a living legend. You score another perfect 300 in the evening's match, the audience cheers, and your serotonin and mood both improve accordingly. The multitude of social situations we encounter can cause our serotonin levels to shift dramatically, along with our moods, depending on where we are, who we're with and what our social status is relative to theirs.

The second difference can be even more difficult to manage, and relates to the incomprehensible social structure that regulates the things we view on our screens. Our brains can't tell that what we see in Hollywood movies, Netflix shows and social media feeds doesn't reflect genuine social structures that we need to somehow relate to. If some person on the other side of the planet happens to have a nicer car, a bigger house, more money, a more attractive appearance, a better skill set and a more successful career than we do, our brains can get the idea that this somehow places them above us in the social order, and this can lower our serotonin, increase our stress and even trigger absolute hopelessness in extreme cases. However, these things can also serve to motivate us. Individuals who possess strong self-esteem, for example, are often motivated by seeing how well others are doing, as it inspires them to want to achieve the same things.

Sometimes people can neutralize this specific but imaginary social status by using the uniquely developed human prefrontal cortex to understand that most of what they see in social media is fake, that what they read in the news isn't necessarily true, that the image of romance pre-sented by Hollywood tends to be rather distorted, and that real life isn't as exciting as a Netflix series. Note that I wrote 'sometimes'. It's incredibly difficult to intellectual-ize instincts that are as old as the ones that regulate social status, but some people have practised doing this and are better at it than others. Age probably plays a part here too, as the prefrontal cortex isn't fully developed until we turn twenty-five years old. This means that the artificial social status messages we're fed every day by social media are more difficult for children and young adults to ignore.

What Grants Us Social Status?

In studies into the abilities of primates to influence their own social status, it has been discovered that this is mainly due to attributes like strength, size and aggression. Human social status is influenced by an incredible array of further variables. Money, appearance, clothing, belongings, age and hiking sticks are just a few examples, but we could also mention more subtle variables, such as the ways we can use our willpower to influence our social status. We can do this by using behavioural tactics, language, body language, subtle signals, cooperation, association with others – i.e. name-dropping – and so on.

I have experienced how social status can influence sero-tonin to a rather ridiculous extent, particularly when using social media. I suffered from acute envy for a long time, to the point where it caused me physical pain to see other people succeed and enjoy greater social status than I did. Their social status seemed to somehow impact mine, though this is obviously not the case – the world is far too big a place for that. Up until about 12,000 years ago, when we were all hunter-gatherers, groups usually consisted of a maximum of 100 individuals and social status was essential for the efficient functioning of the group. But though the chances for survival and growth were greater when belonging to a group, the hierarchy also took its toll because the people at the top would actually be depriving someone lower down of opportunities to feel good, provide for their family and find the best possible mate. These days, our group consists of the billion or so people who post things on social media every day. However ridiculous and absurd this might seem, I used to experience genuine pain and feel like a failure every time I opened an app on my phone and saw people heading away from their gorgeous homes on their yachts with big smiles on their faces. What made me so prone to envy is hard for me to say – perhaps it had something to do with my depressed state, because as the latter receded I began to exhibit more self-esteem, more self-love and less envy.

Receiving compliments and being seen and heard in social contexts are very likely to boost your serotonin. Remember that you can do the same thing for other people – serotonin can be contagious. Give more compliments to the people who are close to you. They will love you for it and be more likely to reciprocate in kind. An interesting aspect of compliments is that their impact depends, to some extent, on the status of the individuals who give them to you. You would respond very differently if Barack Obama, or somebody who enjoys a similar high status, were to give you a compliment, as opposed to a random stranger in the street. So you should always be genuine when giving compliments, and give them with some care, as to do otherwise may devalue their power and purpose.

Now, if compliments can affect our serotonin levels, it seems very likely that the same would be true of criticism. There is an important factor at play here, which I believe has a huge impact on how we receive both compliments and criticism: self-esteem. Let's begin by defining the difference between confidence and self-esteem. The best version of this I've ever heard, which also rings true for me, is this: confidence can be defined as your degree of trust in yourself to carry out various activities. If you've been playing basketball for a long time, won a lot of games and achieved a high level of skill at the sport, you'll probably be very confident about your ability to play basketball. Your self-esteem, on the other hand, reflects how you feel about yourself and how strongly. A person with good self-esteem will genuinely be able to say that they love themselves, that they feel secure about who they are and that they are happy to be the person they are. A person with good self-esteem might respond to a defeat by saying something along the lines of 'Well, I did my best.' Whereas somebody with poor self-esteem might say something like 'I don't deserve to play basketball on this level. I suck!'

Let's get back to how compliments and criticism can affect people differently. If somebody who has strong self-esteem is criticized for how they look, they're unlikely to be too affected by this, as they don't feel that their value lies in their physical appearance, and are generally content with themselves. It's also very clear to me that these individuals don't respond the same way to compliments, either – they tend to treat them as no big deal. They do think they're wonderful as they are, after all, and this is likely to make them less dependent on external recognition. To take the opposite case, somebody who has poor self-esteem could spend their entire life trying to attract attention. The moment they get somebody's attention, their own perceived social status is elevated and they feel fantastic. But if this person were to be criticized for something, their perceived social status would fall to the ground, and their mood along with it. I often describe the life of an individual with poor self-esteem as a roller-coaster ride, which sees them go from abysmal setbacks and despair to blissful moments of harmony and contentedness.

Effect 1: Contentedness

When you feel that your social status is not under threat, this will usually cause you to cease chasing after more of it. In this moment, a sense of contentedness will arise. Being content is an amazing human state, because it allows us to be more present in the moment and enjoy what we already have. If you want to achieve this state, try not to compare yourself to others too much, be content to stay out of the dopamine hunt and consciously practise being appreciative of what you have.

Effect 2: A Good Mood

At what time of year does the average person enjoy the best mood? When are they naturally the happiest? The answer, for most people, is in the spring and summer. And the reason for this, of course, is the sun! Serotonin is also affected by other factors, including exercise, sleep and diet. Of all the substances I'll discuss in this book, I'd have to say that the most important one for you to promote through your lifestyle choices is serotonin. If your mood is stable and good, life will be a whole lot easier for you, and all other changes will be so much easier to bring about! So focus particularly on the following serotonin tools, and make a point of learning how to use them to add serotonin to your Angel's cocktail.

Tool 1: Practise Self-Esteem

The first tool emphasizes overcoming something that I used to struggle with, poor self-esteem, which caused me to experience envy and intense stress whenever I felt that others were enjoying better social status than me. How do you practise self-esteem then? Or, more specifically, how do you practise being less affected by the social status of others?

1. Love yourself! How do you do that? You do it
   the same way many others have chosen not to
   love themselves: by repetition and by maintaining
   a specific focus. When you get something right,

91

give yourself a compliment – pat yourself on the
back and tell yourself how fantastic you are.

2. Stop criticizing yourself for your mistakes.
Simply acknowledge that something went wrong
and decide to learn from it. Then give yourself a
compliment for thinking this way instead of
giving yourself a hard time like you used to!
Self-criticism without learning serves no practical
purpose. It's just a reflexive, learned reaction,
which probably originated in your upbringing,
schooling or some other similar process of
socialization.

3. Poor self-esteem can have its roots in judging
yourself. People who judge themselves tend to
also be more judgemental of others. The bright
side here is that by practising not being
judgemental of others, you can also make
yourself less judgemental of yourself. Practise
this until you don't judge others at all. Human
beings are interesting in that we often judge
others without considering the underlying causes
of their behaviour. If somebody overtakes you
in traffic in a foolish and dangerous way, you're
quite likely to think of them as idiots, without
giving any thought at all to what their reasons
might have been. However, when you overtake
someone else, just as foolishly and dangerously,
you'll usually have some rather easy justification
available for your behaviour – you had to rush to
the hospital, or you were upset because

somebody just broke up with you or you noticed some gravel along the side of the road and had to swerve to avoid spraying oncoming traffic with flying gravel, and so on.

4. A favourite tool of mine, which I have used for a very long time to practise self-love, is to draw a heart with my name inside it. Try it. If it feels uncomfortable or strange to do, that's just a sign that you really need to practise doing it. When I'm in the shower, and the condensation covers the shower door, I fill it with lots of hearts with my name inside them. Loving yourself is the most important thing you can ever do – when you do it, it will make your perceived social status far more robust, and make you less susceptible to being influenced by what other people think of you.

5. Observational meditation is a form of meditation that can help you instinctively value all the thoughts that enter your mind, and can be very effective for boosting serotonin. Sit in a relaxed position, breathe calmly and concentrate on taking deep, slow breaths. Unlike focus meditation, in which you're supposed to concentrate on your breath, in this method, you allow thoughts to enter your mind. The moment they appear, you fly away from them to observe them from a distance without passing judgement. As a succession of your thoughts continue replacing each other, all you do is carry on observing them.

This meditation can help you to respond in the
same way in reality after you finish your meditation,
and make you better at being non-judgemental of
both your own behaviour and that of others.

6. When you catch yourself preparing to feed
yourself a negative message, create a routine in
which you immediately say three positive things
about yourself instead.

7. Every night make an entry in your gratitude
journal about the things you felt you did well and
feel proud about during the day that just went by.
Or thinking about them works just as well.

I love the way serotonin helps me have a positive, balanced mood, and I also love contentedness. I've asked the
following question to almost 50,000 people from all over
the world: when do you feel harmonious and experience
well-being in a way that's entirely detached from any desire
for more or the need to chase after anything (dopamine)?
The answers are strikingly similar: 'When I'm in the woods',
'when I go riding', 'when I'm in my cabin', 'when I'm fishing', 'when I'm by the sea, 'when I go skiing', 'when I play
music', 'when I'm free from all obligations', 'when I exercise', 'when I practise my hobby', 'when I go scuba diving'
or 'when I meditate'. What all these answers have in
common is the fact that they refer to stress-free situations,
and that they seem to involve activities that pose no threat
to one's social status (none of the 50,000 respondents have
ever mentioned competing). Whether all these answers
relate to situations that produce serotonin or not is

impossible to say, of course, but they do relate to the kinds of experiences that serotonin is often associated with.

Tool 2: Dopamine vs Serotonin

The difference between dopamine and serotonin is that dopamine wants to propel you forward in some way. It increases your impulsivity and makes you focus on things external to yourself and your own body. Dopamine is stimulated by the feeling that you need something more to fulfil your needs, and when you've satisfied those needs, serotonin will be released and dampen your impulsivity. A simple example of this would be food. If you're hungry, dopamine will come along to make sure you eat something. As you gradually become full, your dopamine production will slow down, and it will eventually be replaced by serotonin. The term most often used to describe this kind of effect is homeostasis. Because your brain seeks balance, any deviation from the normal state will trigger something, in this case dopamine, that's going to make you want to do something about it. In basic terms, dopamine causes the feeling that you want something you don't already have, while serotonin causes the feeling that you're content with what you already have. These two states play very different roles in our lives, and it's well worth the effort to try to master them both as fully as you possibly can.

You might be more driven by dopamine, or have friends who are, and be familiar with how this drive to try new things never seems to run dry. I'm like that myself.

My brain never stops coming up with new ideas, but, on the other hand, it also loses interest very quickly. It comes up with ambitions that are, honestly speaking, rather insane, and it never gets tired of the hunt. You might be more content in general, and always have been that way – or, at the very least, have friends who are. Of course, every possible combination in between exists too – people vary a lot in how dopamine-driven or serotonin-driven they are. Whether this is innate or learned behaviour has not yet been determined by science. But in any case, the answer doesn't matter that much. What does matter is that you can influence your behaviour thanks to your brain's neuroplasticity (see page 215 for more on this topic).

A dopamine-driven individual can quell their 'craving for the hunt' by reducing their intake of stimuli that trigger dopamine. An example would be to start refraining from moving on to the next dopamine high all the time, and practise enjoying things, being present and experiencing life. I have three primary approaches I use to keep my dopamine in check. The first is to try to reduce obligations as much as possible; the second is to force myself to seek out slow dopamine, like reading a book or working on a practical hobby like fishing or painting; the third is focus meditation – this involves sitting still and counting your breaths or heartbeats.

In my experience of dealing with clients with serotonin-driven personalities, they can increase their 'craving for the hunt' by setting small targets at first, achieving them and then following this up with larger targets that they also go on to achieve – this will often produce some momentum. It's also important to set clear times for when to start and end things, because many of them have a tendency to get caught up in just existing and fail to get done much of what they had planned to do. To-do lists have also proven to be very effective.

It's likely that humans have historically tended to have a better balance between serotonin and dopamine than most of us who attend the dopamine feast that is modern life. The more dopamine you allow yourself to consume, the more of it you will crave, and the longer you run the risk of missing out on the natural sense of contentedness and well-being that serotonin brings.

Tool 3: Daylight

Our third tool is absolutely free. Beyond your walls, beyond your window, beyond your computer screen, outside, you will find one of the most important supplements you could ever take. Recurring studies in northern countries have revealed the same thing: many people's moods drop during the winter months. It's not because we laugh less, or socialize less, or exercise less, or eat worse food – it's because we don't get enough sunlight. Naturally one of the main reasons for this is that the sun barely has time to rise before it begins to set during that time of the year. The second reason is just as important: we tend to stay inside more when it's cold outside. Fortunately the cold doesn't impact the mood-altering effects of the sun – the only factors that matter are the degree of exposure we get and how long we get it. Taking a short walk on a day with blue skies and bright sunshine will feed you more sunlight than a walk of the same length on a cloudy day. Therefore you should take longer walks on cloudy days to make sure you get your fill of sunlight.

What is it the sun does that makes it so important in this regard? Well, the sun affects your daily dose of serotonin. This means that on days when you don't go out into the sunshine, you're making a deliberate choice not to raise your serotonin levels by exposing yourself to the sun. In more technical terms, sunlight reduces serotonin uptake between synapses, which means that it has medical effects similar to those of SSRIs (selective serotonin reuptake inhibitors), a common family of antidepressants. In simpler terms it means that sunlight allows you to 'enjoy' the serotonin you have for longer. Missing out on sunlight for a day now and then isn't such a big deal for most people, but too many days like that in succession can cause people who live in the north to experience a clear difference in mood during the winter months, which can even develop into seasonal affective disorder (SAD) in some people, which causes people to experience depression during the darker months of the year. I love gathering data about myself, because it helps me understand and realize things about me I would never have guessed otherwise! If you, by any chance, happen to share this passion of mine, I'd like to give you this awesome tip: document the amount of sunlight you get every day for a whole year, and record your daily moods on a scale of 1 to 10. You're very likely to identify a trend if you do this, and this will in turn motivate you to begin treating sunlight intake like a mental meal you need each day, one that's every bit as important as breakfast, lunch or dinner.

Your daily serotonin levels will be affected by the light that hits your eyes, which means that the sunlight doesn't actually need to touch your skin. On the other hand, your vitamin D levels are affected by the amount of sunlight that hits your skin. Vitamin D is also important for healthy ageing, anxiety reduction, improved cardiovascular health, maintaining the immune system, improved eyesight and keeping your bones strong. To top it all off, vitamin D also plays an indirect role in your serotonin production. During the darker months of the year, when you're not that likely to dress lightly, I absolutely recommend that you supplement your diet with vitamin D. Good sources include dairy products, other foods with added vitamin D or vitamin pills if your diet is otherwise lacking in vitamin D.

So, to sum this tool up: always make time for a walk, no matter what day or season it is!

Tool 4: Diet

Why is it that the first thing people in Hollywood movies do when they suffer heartbreak is to gorge themselves on ice cream and sweets, and why is a stack of pizza boxes and fast-food leftovers such a common trope when somebody in a movie is going through a crisis? What is it that makes most of us more susceptible to the lure of unhealthy food when we suffer mental difficulties?

One important reason for this is that tryptophan is

indirectly released when we consume carbohydrates. Tryptophan is a substance that the body uses as a building block when producing serotonin. The more carbohydrates we eat, the more tryptophan we get, and thus the more building blocks our brain has access to for making serotonin. It can actually be quite interesting to observe this: if you notice that you're eating an increasing amount of carbohydrates, this could indicate a shortage of tryptophan, which might in turn also mean that your mood is less balanced or gloomier. If that feeling sticks around, it's important that you address it. Mental imbalances will only become more difficult to manage and recover from the longer you allow them to go on.

Let's take a closer look at tryptophan. It's an amino acid that's used as a building block for serotonin production, one that we source from the food we eat. If you're not eating enough tryptophan, this will impact your capacity for serotonin production. The foods that are richest in tryptophan include turkey, chicken, fish, green bananas, oats, cheese, nuts, seeds and milk. You can also buy tryptophan as a dietary supplement – the most powerful source in this context is believed to be St John's wort supplements. However, you should always consult your doctor before introducing a new dietary supplement – this is especially important if you're already taking other medication, particularly antidepressants.

Another interesting aspect of serotonin is that 90–95 per cent of all the serotonin in your body is in your stomach. It was long believed that there was no connection between serotonin in the gut and serotonin in the brain, as it wasn't believed to penetrate the blood-brain barrier. An interesting study from 2019, by Karen-Anne McVey Neufeld and others, showed, however, that a connection may exist and that it could be regulated via the vagus nerve. In the last few years, we've seen a deluge of studies on the impact of our microbiome and the brain–gut connection on our mental health. Although these studies are rather complex, the information they provide is simple: the things we eat directly impact our mental health. What, then, should we be eating? The answer is a diverse diet. Different kinds of food will maintain and provide sustenance for different kinds of digestive bacteria, and the more you have of the good digestive bacteria, the better off you will be. You may decide to use probiotics, although their documented effects are limited. Avoid fast food, processed foods, fast carbohydrates and white sugar, and increase your intake of slow carbohydrates from fruit, vegetables and whole grains. One effect of low serotonin levels that can seem rather frightening is that, as I mentioned, they can cause us to eat more fast carbohydrates. They can also cause a higher uptake of the sweetener aspartame, which is bad news in this case, as this sweetener has been shown to contribute to reduced levels of not only serotonin, but also of dopamine and noradrenaline. Bit of a vicious cycle, eh?

My suggestion is to pay attention whenever you feel the urge to eat fast carbohydrates. Learn to recognize this urge and learn to stop it in time, before it sends you shambling off to the shops for snacks, sweets and carbonated drinks like some remote-controlled zombie. Once you've learned to recognize the signs, I'd like to recommend some other options you can use to quell the cravings: carrots, nuts, chocolate with over 80 per cent cocoa solids and sugar-snap peas. Those are my go-tos in moments of weakness.

Tool 5: Mindfulness

You've heard of this concept a million times by now. Mindfulness is a magical practice, a skill to master and a method that can bring you the ultimate sense of contentedness. I've heard about so many people who have completely turned their lives around just by practising mindfulness. The opposite of mindfulness is often referred to as context switching. This allows you to do several things at once, which means that you're spending most of your time on the way somewhere else, either physically or mentally. Now if context switching is the opposite of mindfulness, is it useful? Well, it's certainly useful in the sense that it can allow you to get a lot of stuff done, which is one measure of success, after all. The problem is that context switching seems to have a negative impact on our ability to be present in the moment. Is being present important, then? I'd have to say that being present trumps context switching, because it's only when we're present that we're able to take in the world around us through our senses.

An everyday example of context switching might be cooking. Somebody who has trained their brain to do a lot of context switching will find it challenging to cook the food step by step. The context switcher might find themselves also doing dishes, watching a TV show, organizing their spice rack and preparing lunch boxes for the next day. This person will miss out on the actual experience of cooking. What this automatically brings to mind for me is a passionate Italian who invests a great deal of passion in the actual process of cooking – somebody like that would be unlikely to be switching contexts a lot, and thus, they embody the mindful attitude quite well.

Another example is when you meet new people. Somebody who is fully present will ask a new person questions, get to know them in depth, empathize with them and show genuine interest in them. I'm sure you can relate to both the experience of meeting somebody who's fully present and the experience of meeting someone whose gaze, thoughts, body and actions seem to keep roaming all over the place.

Next, a third example. Your emotions are mainly produced by two things: your thoughts, on the one hand, and your sensory input, i.e. the things you experience through your senses of hearing, touch, sight, smell and taste, on the other. All these trigger the release of serotonin, endocannabinoids, dopamine and other chemicals. By consciously experiencing your sensations, you can fully sample the chemistry of your emotions.

Like anything else, presence can be developed through practice, and we can all get better at being present. The best part of all this is that you're free to start right now. Read slower. Enjoy taking in the knowledge you're being given, enjoy the warmth and comfort of your surroundings, and enjoy your coffee. Congratulations! You've just practised being present, and your brain has made some progress towards experiencing more emotions, and stronger ones too.

A good long-term strategy for practising being present is to focus on one particular sense each day. For example, you could focus on smell on Monday, and deliberately choose to take in the scent of a banana, the glue in your wallpaper, your own skin, somebody who walks by and so on.

If you already feel fully present in your five basic senses, I have some challenges prepared for you, which are inspired by recent advances in sensory science: pressure, temperature, muscle tensions, pain, balance, thirst, hunger and time.

Now, some of you might feel like objecting at this point, because you don't want to give up any of your efficiency. Is it really possible to train the brain to do just one single thing at a time? None of this stuff is at all black and white, of course, but you can't expect your brain to spend all week at work context switching at full throttle, and then be able to pull on the brake at the weekend to a state of effortless, full and absolute focus on your presence of mind and your senses. Nobody can do that, except maybe a rare few superheroes. Balance is key here. Rather than running at full throttle, take it down a notch and practise being present at work too. You may find to your surprise that you do your job even better. Experience the people, the successes, the fun, the progress and all the other emotions available there. You spend enough time at your job, so make sure to enjoy it as much as you can!

My own reliable 'handbrake' trick is to go to Abisko just before my five-week summer holiday kicks in. Abisko is, without a doubt, one of the most beautiful places in Sweden. Located in the most northern part of the country it proudly presents itself with massive mountains, incredible views and water so clear you can see the bottom of the stream and even drink directly from it if you so desire. After spending just a single week there without my smartphone, my brain comes to a full halt, and the rest of my summer is no challenge at all. If I don't make it there, it can take my brain four to five weeks just to wind down, and by that time I need it to be getting back into gear! If I want to achieve the same effect for the weekend, I consciously start to wind down at lunchtime on the Friday, and I schedule half an hour of meditation at the end of my workday. Setting my phone aside at the weekend, on top of this, will ensure that my brain is fully ready to transition from mostly context switching to mostly being present.

Tool 6: Harness The Power of Your Mind

I know that I've already mentioned this, but I'm going to go ahead and repeat myself, because it's absolutely vital that you take this in: memories of events can trigger similar emotions as the events themselves. A memory, in other words, releases the same or similar substances as the actual experience that is being remembered. What makes this so hugely important is the fact that most people I encounter don't choose their thoughts; they simply allow themselves to be influenced by whatever happens around them, and the kinds of things we tend to be surrounded by in our society are more often harmful than not in terms of their influence on us. Positive news doesn't sell as well as bad news. During coffee breaks, conversation tends towards the negative rather than the positive, because bringing up a negative subject is likely to achieve a greater impact and attract more attention to the person who's speaking. On social media, everything looks too good to be true. However, our brains seem unable to realize this – they seem to believe that we should be comparing ourselves to the phoney images we're presented with on social media 99 per cent of the time. Comparing ourselves to them can cause us to become overly self-critical, which is far from a good outcome. Becoming aware of your thoughts and learning to control them are absolutely essential steps for successful self-leadership – and they will set you on the path to being able to choose how you want to feel. My guess is that you'll choose to feel fantastic and well balanced.

Tool 7: Exercise, Diet, Sleep and Meditation

Exercise, diet, sleep and meditation all offer excellent ways of boosting your serotonin. Since these four factors can potentially produce whole Angel's cocktails of their own, I've chosen to address them in greater detail later on. Think of them as 'super ingredients' in your Angel's cocktail (page 171).

Tool 8: Stress

This tool is less about how to produce serotonin than it is about how you can indirectly improve your serotonin balance by avoiding chronic stress. And although this tool may be indirect, it's possibly the most powerful one of all. Let's begin by examining the most common reasons for imbalanced serotonin in humans:

- Chronic physical pain
- Strong emotional pain, resulting from anything from bullying to the loss of a loved one
- Illness
- Inflammation
- Negative thought patterns
- Malnutrition, including tryptophan deficiency
- Poor gut health
- Lack of exercise
- Lack of sunlight

It's interesting to note that stress can be a dominant factor in more than half the causes listed above. Physical pain can cause stress, emotional pain can cause stress, illness can cause stress, inflammation is stressful for the body, and negative thought patterns can cause stress. In my years as a coach, I've met many clients who weren't too severely impacted during the immediate aftermath of the loss of a loved one; it took two to three months for the emotional impact to develop fully. Struggling with chronic stress for months or years on end can cause effects just like these and lead to full-on depression. Interestingly there appears to be no connection between low serotonin levels and depression, which is something of a mystery when you consider the fact that antidepressants that affect the serotonin system seem to help so many depression patients. Although stress can be fantastic, chronic stress is one of the single most negative influences on our mental and physical well-being. It's as though we all carry a potentially dark force within ourselves, which has a greater potential to negatively influence our mental health than anything else. But before we move on to investigating stress and cortisol, let's sum up this chapter on serotonin.

Serotonin – A Summary

I've come to realize that contentedness and harmony are the most important foundations for your Angel's cocktail. All other positive emotional states, including euphoria, love, motivation, rewards, excitement and arousal, tend to be temporary and come and go, whereas contentedness and harmony have the potential to be a lot more stable in a person's life. These temporary emotional states should be experienced in full, and often, of course, but a life that emphasizes nothing but short-term emotional states runs the risk of ending up feeling like one big roller-coaster ride. On the other hand, if you can use serotonin as the base for your Angel's cocktail, this will give you some solid ground to return to when the fairground closes for the night. So, set the foundation for your Angel's cocktail by avoiding chronic stress, exercising, meditating, getting plenty of sunlight, eating a healthy diet, building self-esteem and practising being content rather than constantly seeking stimulation.

Cortisol

Focus, Excitement or Panic?

Let's begin by going over the benefits of stress, and its three main components (cortisol, adrenaline and noradrenaline), and then move on to what happens when you suddenly come face to face with a sabretooth tiger or a honking car.

Cortisol is perhaps the most important hormone in the human body. In stressful situations your adrenal glands release cortisol into your bloodstream, which in turn triggers a huge release of glucose. This glucose, or sugar, gives you the energy you need to handle your stressful situation. Cortisol plays a vital role in its own right, as it balances the immune system's activity during inflammation, by providing the immune system with sugar to fuel it, and by acting as a short-term anti-inflammatory.

Adrenaline, in turn, increases the heart rate, directs blood flow to the muscles (this is why you feel yourself trembling), and finally relaxes your airways to allow you to get more oxygen to your muscles, so you can punch harder or run faster.

Noradrenaline provides a cognitive boost, heightening your focus and attention.

Together, these substances set the stage for saving you by initiating one of three modes: flight, fight or freeze.

Once you've realized that the sabretooth tiger has seen you, you'll stop standing still and make your escape far quicker than you would normally be able to. This mechanism has kept our species alive for hundreds of thousands of years.

Do you remember our apple picker Duncan from 25,000 years ago? He was hungry and needed to find food, but it wasn't dopamine alone that sent him off looking for something to eat. It was cortisol and dopamine working together. The purpose of cortisol in this context is to get you to take action, to move from one location to another. Cortisol triggers an uneasy feeling in you, an anxious state that you won't want to stay in. So when Duncan wakes up and realizes that he's hungry, it will be cortisol that first gives him the feeling that he has to get up and move. The dopamine that follows the cortisol in this process had Duncan visualizing wild apples and imagining how tasty they would be. Dopamine can be likened to a magical force dragging you towards a target – the feeling it gives you is far more pleasant than the one you get from cortisol. These two forces combined to coax Duncan from his comfortable straw bed and led him to the treacherous terrain where he arrived at the apple tree and finally found what he was looking for. In highly simplified terms, these are our two driving forces in life (avoiding pain and seeking pleasure). It's cortisol's role to make us seek to avoid pain, most often expressed as 'I have to . . .' Dopamine, on the other hand, is the driving force that makes us seek pleasure, which is more likely to make us say 'I want to . . .' Both will get you from point A to point B, but the experiences involved will be very different. Think of the difference between 'I want to go for a walk' and 'I have to go for a walk'. Or what about 'I want to go to work' vs 'I have to go to work'? The whole feeling is entirely different, wouldn't you agree? It could be as simple as redefining your 'have-tos' as 'want-tos'. This makes most things a whole lot easier.

Think of stress as something that arises from the gap between what you have and what you wish you had. If you lament your weight on a daily basis, it will most likely cause you stress. This may eventually motivate you to go to the gym – but it will also keep you from achieving the best possible results from your exercise. However, if you can successfully convert this dissatisfaction into a source of drive and an emotional target, the gap between what you have and what you wish you had will become a source of dopamine instead.

As you can tell, the relationship between dopamine and cortisol is a brilliant and fantastic aspect of the human condition. But, as is so often the case, there is also a downside. This incredible mechanism, you see, has also contributed to humanity's rapid creation of a society that produces so many novel and completely unnecessary sources of stress. Here are some examples:

- News stories that paint the world in an unfavourable light
- Refined sugar that causes blood sugar spikes
- Social media that defines how we view the world
- Social media that causes us to compare ourselves to bizarre social structures
- A business culture that relies so heavily on deadlines
- A culture that rates performance over happiness

- A culture in which goals matter more than being present
- Loud noises, if you live in a city
- Indirect stress caused by pollution, if you live in a city or close to a main road
- A work–life balance people struggle with
- A digital world that robs our children of their dopamine
- A digital world that robs us of our dopamine
- Helicopter parenting rather than offering to help, which produces children who demand stimulation
- Smartphone notifications
- The expectation of constant availability
- Loneliness and social isolation
- A lack of natural reasons to move around
- Inadequate pension schemes that make us worry about getting old
- An attention-based culture that excessively promotes negative speech

I'm sorry if just reading this list made you feel stressed. However, if you go back and look at it again, you'll realize that 25,000 years ago, most of these things simply weren't valid reasons to feel stressed. People could certainly experience stress as a result of their fear of becoming ill or being harmed, but in general their list of potential stressors was incredibly short. Why do we feel so bad if our lives are so good? The fact that cortisol is constantly vying for our attention and dopamine is always trying to lure us with its many temptations is obviously part of the answer.

Now, I'd like to clarify something: limited amounts of stress aren't just pleasant, they're fantastic! Stress can make us feel alive, so we can feel our blood pulsing through our veins. Sometimes the focus we gain from the stress hormone noradrenaline can make us feel invincible, and the adrenaline rushing through us before we perform a challenging exercise at the gym can make us feel both strong and alive. Ask any experienced skydiver – they'll usually admit to actively seeking out stress. They're addicted to the adrenaline rush it gives them, and that's why they keep challenging themselves to use smaller parachutes and make more dangerous dives. Stress in small amounts is the elixir of life, and a great source of energy.

Personally I love cold-water bathing. There are few experiences that produce the same intense stress as cold-water baths. It's the same with fasting, which also exerts stress on your body and brain. I could never choose to live a life without any stress. On the other hand, I would be just as reluctant to choose a life of chronic stress, whether that be intense, long-lasting stress or low-level constant stress. Unfortunately, although most of us are reluctant to admit it or even realize it, most humans suffer long-term stress levels that are quite literally unhealthy. This can have a series of detrimental effects on our mental and physical health. Some examples:

- Chronic pain
- Digestive issues
- Cardiovascular disease
- Memory impairment

- Loss of lust for life
- Excess weight
- Insomnia
- Lethargy
- Recurring colds
- Weakened immune system

Now, wait a minute – didn't I just claim that cortisol strengthens the immune system? Well, it does do that, but only in the short term. If the stress becomes persistent, it has the opposite effect and becomes harmful. You should read this section particularly carefully, because what I'm about to share with you will probably give you new and important insights.

When we become injured or cut, this causes an inflammation and red swellings appear at the site of the injury. White blood cells are recruited and produced, and pro-inflammatory cytokines (a kind of signalling molecule that the cells in our bodies use to communicate) are produced by our triggered immune systems. One effect of these cytokines is that they can cause other cells in our immune systems to begin converting the building block tryptophan (yep, the same one as for serotonin) into kynurenine. Kynurenine, in turn, can be further converted into substances like quinolinic acid and kynurenic acid, which are both potentially neurotoxic (i.e. toxic to the brain), and can contribute to a depressed mood in the longer term. The next part is the important bit, however! Inflammation isn't exclusively caused by physical injuries; it can also be triggered by psychological stress. Eventually psychological stress can cause mild chronic inflammation in the body (the exact mechanisms of this still elude science), and thus bring about states in which our serotonin levels drop.

If you've been keeping up so far, you will realize at this point that stress has a dual negative impact on our serotonin and mental health. Inflammation doesn't merely rob us of tryptophan, which is an important building block for serotonin production, the stolen goods are even handed over to a process that produces neurotoxins! Why, then, would the body choose to use its tryptophan to fuel the inflammatory process rather than for producing serotonin? The answer is simple: your survival is far more important than the stability and quality of your mood. In other words, the reason I wouldn't like to live with chronic stress is that I want my serotonin balance to remain intact!

What exactly is chronic stress? It can be defined as a state in which stress keeps you constantly wound up, and normal rest doesn't significantly help you unwind. The duration required for stress to be considered 'chronic' seems to vary a lot from one study to the next, but my estimate of the average duration would be somewhere between one and four months. This means that if you were to feel as though you were being constantly, mercilessly hounded by a sabretooth tiger for four months, you'd qualify as chronically stressed and have to do something about it.

Somebody might object that they have been chronically stressed for years without suffering any ill effects, and reckon that they might as well go on that way. In all likelihood, though, their chronic stress is going to cause them health issues at some point in the future, even if there's nothing to suggest any such problem at present. Two years ago, I became chronically stressed. In January everything seemed fine. I was travelling around the world, giving twenty-five lectures and participating in numerous interviews, recordings and the like. Within a single week I lectured in six countries on two continents. The pace I was keeping wasn't even causing me much stress, as I was doing a job I knew well and felt comfortable doing. A month or so later, the Covid-19 panic closed everything down. For me this meant that all my bookings for the rest of the year evaporated within a week. There was no future income in sight for me or for my team of ten people. But I still felt confident that I could deal with this, since I tend to pivot well. A week later, I had reorganized our business: we were going all in on social media, launching our online training classes at HeadGain.com, and building a digital recording studio. We hadn't done any of this before, and there weren't really any experts to consult with, as video conferences and digital lectures were hardly in use yet at the time, so we simply had to read up on it, fiddle away and work it all out through trial and error. It ended up costing somewhere between one and two hundred thousand euros and taking us six months, but I was confident that it would be worth it. Rather than slowing down, like many others were doing at the time, I chose, as I almost always do, to go for broke and gear up instead. My plan was for us to exit the pandemic stronger than we had been going in. And we did incredibly well. If we could just increase our pace over the summer, we would be ready to launch lots of new products and services by the autumn, and that would surely save the whole business. However, everything was about to change over just two days, because of two separate disasters that I had in no way seen coming.

The first of these disasters happened in early June. My son came running into my home office, shouting, 'Mummy has fallen down!' I dropped everything and ran out to her. On the stairs, outside the house, Maria lay, barely able to speak. She was mumbling something I could hardly make out. 'I've had a stroke.' Panic, tears, ambulance ride, confusion . . . I wasn't told anything, and I wasn't allowed into the hospital with her because of the pandemic. I noticed a missed call from an unlisted number, which meant that the hospital had probably tried to reach me, and the fact they were calling me instead of my wife made me think it couldn't be good news. I froze and just stared at my phone. After what felt like an eternity, they tried my number again, and the slowest voice in human history explained to me that Maria was going to be OK, that her stroke had probably been caused by Covid-19, and that she was facing a long process of recovery.

Two days later, I discovered the next disaster. It turned out that one of my good friends, let's call him Curt, who had been helping me with my company finances, had been systematically mismanaging the business. I only found out about it after Curt explained to me that we had been denied the state payroll assistance funding for the pandemic. When I called the Swedish Agency for Economic and Regional Growth to find out if this was really true, I was told that they had never received an application from us. I sensed that something was amiss and carried on digging. This was an absolute catastrophe. I won't get into all the details, but suffice to say that over the course of the next three days, we went from being what looked to be a flourishing, functional business to losing our business tax licence and discovering that our bank account was practically empty. I can't possibly describe the stress I experienced.

I was left with only two options: I could either work harder than ever before or lose everything I had worked for. We had no money left, our rainy-day fund was gone and the company was in a miserable state. We weren't bringing in any money, my wife had suffered a stroke and I had already had to pick up the pace in order to write, record and build everything I needed for our digital pivot.

The day after her stroke, a success coaching business was scheduled to visit me at the JP-Manor, outside Västerås in Sweden, to do an all-day shoot of my new digital course. Did I have any choice? Could I call them and cancel? No, the only option open to me was to keep moving forward. Despite all my knowledge of self-leadership and the mechanisms of stress, I had too many simultaneous challenges to balance, and ended up struggling. I was meditating, exercising and sleeping well, which probably ultimately saved me, but my chronic stress became quite obvious before too long. Just two months after her stroke, at some point in August, I began to develop carpal tunnel syndrome in my arms, nerve pain that emanated from my shoulders to my fingers. I also developed iritis, an inflammation of the eye that indicated that my immune system was attacking me. All these things were piling up on top of me at a time when what I needed more than anything was to solve the issues my business was facing and keep my family afloat. I ended up pushing myself way too far, and I'm confident that I shaved a couple of years off my life in doing so.

By February 2022, Maria was nearly fully recovered, almost entirely thanks to her own outstanding self-leadership skills. She's definitely my role model in that regard – it was an astounding achievement! My own health was back on track too. My staff and four of my friends had come to my assistance during the summer to help me get the business sorted out. We eventually regained our tax licence in November. We launched HeadGain.com, my digital training platform, with all my courses, 500 video clips and enough writing to fill three books in October. By February, the site had more than a thousand users world-wide. We made a big splash in social media that year, and my team and I went from 5,000 YouTube followers to 200,000, from 5,000 Instagram followers to 145,000, and from zero to two million TikTok followers, making the account the seventh biggest in Sweden. We had built a world-class digital studio, and in February I gave a story-telling lecture for Google USA. This would end up giving me my big break in the USA – the place where most lec-turers from Sweden can only dream of finding success. As you can probably tell, 2020 and 2021 have gone down in my life as some of the worst and some of the best years ever. The experience was more than challenging, but I learned a great deal. I'm also very confident that if it hadn't been for my self-leadership skills, I would simply have crumbled.

There's a wonderful metaphor that serves as my guiding light in self-leadership, and it goes like this: imagine that you're a gardener. You've made yourself a spectacular garden and filled it with beautiful flowers. The roses symbolize serotonin and the tulips symbolize dopamine. You also grow flowers that represent testosterone, oestrogen and progesterone. Oxytocin is a handsome, lanky sunflower. You're quite proud of your gorgeous lush garden. Suddenly, one day, when you're working away by the rose bushes, you feel a drop of water land on your arm. You smile, and think, *Finally, some rain!* You go inside and stand by the window with a cup of tea, watching the rain pour down on your garden. You know that this is just what it needs to be healthy, just like you need small doses of stress from time to time to be fully well. However, the persistence of this rain soon becomes concerning to you, as it carries on pouring down for weeks on end. It won't stop! It rains for a whole month! You look out at your garden, which is just a faded memory of its former glory by now. It looks withered. It's muddy, dead and grey. This is the metaphorical effect of prolonged stress. We know that chronic stress can directly and indirectly affect your six substances. It's really no surprise that we don't feel our best after struggling with chronic stress for years on end.

Now, can you guess the most common solutions people come up with to reinvigorate themselves after something like that? Shopping, travelling, fine dining, cinema visits, redecorating and renovating their homes. But, as soon as you've done one of these things, the stress and negativity will be right back and you'll feel just as miserable as before. Going back to the garden analogy, in a panic, you, the gardener, run right out to plant new rose bushes, new tulips and new hibiscus bushes. For a short while, the garden will come back to life, before succumbing once more to the never-ending rain.

The only thing that will do any good in the long run is reducing the amount of rain, i.e. the negative chronic stress that's affecting you. The effects of choosing to do this can be glorious and awesome. What happens to your garden when the sun comes back, when the flower beds dry up and the rain only returns for brief spells between sunny days? Your garden will recover on its own. You'll be standing there at your window, watching your flowers come back to life, and seeing all the colour and lushness return to the garden without having to put in any effort at all. It's just the same in life.

I quite often meet people who are struggling with their moods. They might express it as a lack of basic happiness or say they feel a depression coming on. Whenever I meet someone like this, I usually first recommend that they map out their negative stress, and systematically reduce it until it feels manageable or goes away completely. Some people make pretty drastic decisions to achieve this, like moving out of the city, while others resolve minor stressors, like old conflicts that have festered for too long.

Have you ever considered the fact that negative stress doesn't really exist as such, and that it's really a matter of how you interpret a certain situation? With the exception of noisy urban environments and toxins causing stress, what actually makes stress negative is your own perception of the experience. The good news here is that armed with this realization, you can rid yourself of almost all the negative stress in your life eventually. Is this easy to do? Not really. But is it worth the effort? Absolutely!

Inflammation causes depressive symptoms, and many people who struggle with clinical depression also suffer from inflammation, according to findings by Marlena Colasanto of Toronto University and Emanuele Felice Osimo at Cambridge University. An interesting effect that I've noticed in myself and my clients is that a common cold can often cause depressed emotions to come to the surface. This isn't too surprising really, when you consider that colds are caused by inflammation in the body. However, it's important to mention that inflammation is a phenomenon that plays an absolutely vital role in the body's capacity to eliminate hostile micro organisms, clear out dead cells, mend damaged tissue and contain infections. It's the undesirable, mild, chronic inflammation caused by chronic stress that forms the base for a Devil's cocktail – something you should try to avoid getting too much of. The best way to avoid this undesirable form of inflammation is to get good exercise, eat a healthy diet and reduce the negative stress in your life, so that your body won't get the idea that it's constantly having to stave off some threat or other.

Now that we have a better understanding of the nature of stress, as well as of its positive and potentially negative effects, it's time to go over some practical tools we can use to produce or reduce stress as the need arises.

Tool 1: The Stress Map

As I mentioned at the very beginning of the book, the stress map was the first and most important tool I created to help me overcome depression. Although I created it, the person who inspired me to do so was my self-leadership guru and wife, Maria. I spent the entire summer of 2016 in bed, crying inconsolably. I felt no desire to do anything. Even eating felt pointless. Nothing had any meaning to me, and I was consumed by an uncontrollable darkness that would permit me only to weep. We were running a summer café, and one of my favourite singer-songwriters came to perform for our guests. I made my way out of the house to listen, standing far away so nobody would see me, but I couldn't feel a thing. At some point in early August, Maria came to me. She sat down on the edge of the bed, and told me, 'David, I'm taking responsibility for everything. For our three children, for cooking our meals, for keeping the house clean, running the café, the business, the farmhouse, our staff. All of it. You don't need to do any of it.' When she rose to leave, I didn't feel anything in particular, but I did stop crying a week or so later. Four weeks after that, I began to feel relieved, and my motivation was starting to slowly return to me, something I hadn't felt in a long time. I realized that what she was doing for me was stopping the rain from pouring down on my garden. She removed my stress, which had an enormous, almost incomprehensible effect on me, and, because of that, I was eventually able to return to work, although I would probably have been wise to spend another year or two recovering. And, as I wrote at the beginning of the book, it was then that I went to Gothenburg to give a lecture, where I received feedback for getting a detail wrong, which in turn caused me to visit my doctor, who told me in no uncertain terms that I was literally in the process of killing myself. These two factors combined motivated me to overcome the dark moods that had troubled me for most of my life, and my first step towards achieving this end was the stress map. The method is relatively simple, and I recommend it to everybody, regardless of whether they subjectively feel stressed in the current phases of their lives.

Step 1: Write down all your stressors on a sheet of paper.

Step 2: Assign each of your stressors to one of the following categories: *Can be eliminated, Can be resolved* and *Don't know.*

Can be eliminated: this is where you put everything in your life that causes you stress and which you immediately know you could remove from your life.

Can be resolved: this is where you put everything in your life that causes you stress but which you can help yourself to live with until it no longer causes you stress.

Don't know: this is where you put things you don't know how to address at the moment.

Can be eliminated	Can be resolved	Don't know

Ten Examples of 'Can be eliminated'

1. Break off ties with friends and relatives who consistently make you feel bad about yourself.
2. Give up smoking or drinking.
3. Turn off the notifications on your smartphone.
4. Sell something you barely use but think of as a financial burden.
5. Find a new job or position.
6. Delete apps that make you feel bad about yourself.
7. Stop booking meetings without scheduling breaks afterwards – give yourself some breathing space!
8. Avoid tight deadlines.

9. Stop taking responsibility for things you don't need to be taking responsibility for.
10. Avoid taking on too many commitments, from boardroom positions to membership of the allotment association.

Ten Examples of 'Can be resolved'

1. You and your partner disagree on something. Practise being accepting of others.
2. Conflicts. Practise viewing this as an opportunity for growth instead.
3. You've set your goals too high. Break them down into smaller milestones.
4. Children's shoes in the hall. Does this really matter, in the grand scheme of things?
5. Self-critical thoughts. Counter each critical thought by having three positive thoughts about yourself.
6. Difficulty being present in the moment. Remove some of your fast-dopamine sources.
7. Poor confidence. Arrange small wins for yourself and celebrate each one!
8. Sleep. Use the tips on pages 171–173.
9. Feeling trapped. Read about false belief under Tool 8 in this chapter on stress (page 132).
10. Negative mindset. Read about focus questions on page 191.

Examples of 'Don't know'

The stressors you list here are harder to provide examples of, as they tend to vary a lot between different individuals. Usually, if something ends up on this list, it's because you can't see the solution yourself, because you don't have the courage to resolve the situation or because you lack the tools needed to do so. However strange and unlikely this may sound, 99 per cent of all problems can be solved, either in the conventional sense or by altering your perspective on them to the point where they simply cease to be problems. An example of something I put on my own 'Don't know' list was my fear of conflicts, which I realized I could change my perspective on, by seeing them as challenges and learning experiences and then addressing them one at a time. Another example was my lack of courage to be myself, which I solved with the use of focus questions (see page 191). In this case, I changed my initial question from 'how can I avoid standing out?' to 'how can I be an inspiration to others?' This single change made an enormous difference in my life.

Tool 2: Meditation

Sometimes my lecturing schedule can get very tight. On occasion I've had to travel by helicopter to a waiting taxi, and then arrive with just five minutes to spare. Now, if all the time I have to get ready is five minutes, I make a point of not spending that time preparing what I'm going to say.

What I do instead is meditate. Meditation has many bene-fits, but I'm bringing it up here because of its potential to lower your cortisol levels, which will help you think more clearly and make you more in tune with your emotions. Five minutes later, I open my eyes, put my microphone on and walk on to the stage – relaxed and controlled. I'll give you some tips on how to meditate on page 179.

Tool 3: Oxytocin

Oxytocin is released when you feel stressed, probably to help dampen the effects of the stress. What you can do is help this process along by hugging somebody, receiving a massage, performing a gratitude meditation or using my absolute favourite tool, which I've already mentioned: pull out your smartphone, and look at something that fills you with feel-ings of empathy and love. I usually look at pictures of my kids. I mentioned earlier that your oxytocin levels are nega-tively affected by chronic stress. In a study published in 2014 in the *Journal of Psychiatric Research*, it was discovered that women who suffer from depression have particularly low levels of oxytocin compared to women who aren't depressed. As we learned earlier, chronic stress can cause depression.

Tool 4: Exercise

Exercise improves your stress tolerance. Personally, I don't think there's any way I could keep up with the high pace of my life without physical exercise. All it takes is for me to go without exercise for a week or so, and I'll immediately feel my stress tolerance weaken. Remember that extremely intense physical exercise can actually cause more stress than you might need. If you're already feeling very stressed, a less intense exercise routine might be a better fit for you.

Tool 5: Move About

I've spent most of my life training people in presentation skills and communication. One thing that almost everybody who gets stressed in these situations has in common is that they respond by either freezing and hiding in a corner with their laser pointer, or entering flight mode and pacing back and forth across the stage. In both cases you can easily reduce your stress levels by planning out your movements on the stage ahead of time. Make a plan for where to stand and how to move when you'll be saying different things. Plan when to point at your slides and place props some distance away, so that you have to move to fetch them. The more relaxed you can make your motions, the less stressed you'll actually feel. The same is true in life: move about – it'll work wonders for your stress levels.

Tool 6: Breathing

One of the single most powerful tools you can use to alleviate temporary stress is your breathing. If you switch over to taking just a few long breaths each minute, this breathing pace will signal to your brain that all is well and that you're out of danger. The number of breaths to go for will vary depending on your lung volume and other factors, but somewhere between six and eight breaths a minute will usually provide the most calming effects in the shortest time. You can try this right away – just set a timer for one minute and count your breaths. Focus on long inhalations and long exhalations. Don't hold your breath. Instead, regulate the length of your inhalations and exhalations. You'll probably feel calmer after the minute is up. If you really want to experience a powerful contrast, try the breathing exercise that is coming up later on in this chapter (page 142).

Another wonderful breathing tool is the physiological sigh. Breathe in twice, very quickly, to expand your lungs as much as you possibly can, and then exhale very slowly, to compress your lungs. After this, finish with an audible sigh, almost like a groan. Repeat this five or six times. The difference between this tool and simply breathing slowly is that the physiological sigh will expand your lungs even more, and allow you to more effectively eject carbon dioxide from your body. The reason we add an audible sigh at the end of the exhale is that the vagus nerve passes very close to the larynx. The vagus nerve is your most important nerve for calm and relaxation, and when it is activated the parasympathetic nervous system transmits signals to more or less all your organs, to inform them that all is well. Some noises you can make with your vocal cords stimulate the vagus nerve more effectively than others, and the audible sigh or groan is one such sound. This is also partly the reason some people use mantras like 'om' when meditating.

Breathing tools are an excellent way of returning control of your brain to your prefrontal cortex, the part of the brain where your will and intentionality reside. It can be difficult to rely on mental techniques for regaining control when you're suffering from uncontrollable stress or anxiety. In those situations, it's far better to kick-start the process with a relaxing breathing tool, and then proceed to use mental tools to break your thought patterns or alter your behaviour. For example, in a stressful situation, you might begin by breathing calmly for two minutes (physiological technique), and then go on to speaking to yourself in the third person (mental technique). See page 79 for guidance on how to do this.

Tool 7: Alter Your Perspective

Did you know that your physiological responses to nervousness and to positive anticipation are practically identical? It might sound crazy to you but it's true. Plenty of studies have shown that you can successfully redefine your experience of stress and frame it as positive rather than negative. To take a real-world example, let's look at a study by Alison Wood Brooks, which was published in the *Journal of Experimental Psychology*. In this experiment participants were asked to sing the Journey song 'Don't Stop Believin''. One group was told to tell themselves 'I am anxious' before singing, and another group was told to tell themselves 'I am excited'

before singing. The difference this made for the participants' experiences was huge. The individuals in the group
who had told themselves they were excited sang better, felt
more relaxed and had more fun. Similar effects have been
demonstrated in people taking important exams or giving
presentations – if people frame their experiences as exciting rather than nerve-wracking, they perform a lot better!

Tool 8: False Beliefs

Do you remember how difficult you found all the different
procedures that go into driving when you took your first
driving lesson? You have to master the accelerator, clutch,
indicators, mirrors, gearbox and so on. However, you
probably also remember that six months later driving
already seemed like second nature. Perhaps you don't have
a driving licence, but I'm sure you can recall something
else you had to learn that required huge amounts of focus
at first, but soon became so habitual to you that you didn't
even need to consciously think about it to do it. The function that automates learned processes and integrates them
into our muscle memory is amazing, but unfortunately
there is a similar function that automates our emotions,
and this doesn't always work out as well for us. When we're
born, we don't yet know when to feel a certain way, or
what to feel, and our parents may not always successfully
teach us what to feel and when to feel it – we will often
need to complement our learning from home with first-
hand experience of various situations.

Until the age of thirty-five, I carried around the false beliefs that I was ugly and that girls were frightening. How on earth does somebody arrive at such bizarre 'beliefs' and emotions? When I tried to figure out how it had all started, I realized that the origin of this belief was a school party in fifth grade. A tiny disco ball hung down from the ceiling, the stereo blasted out 'It Must Have Been Love' by Roxette, the girls were all giggling in a corner and the boys were huddled together in a different corner. This was going to be the night when I would ask my great love, Maria, to dance with me. After much hesitation, and countless refills of popcorn, I crossed the dance floor on what felt like the legs of a newborn elk calf. Time froze. I cleared my throat. She turned around and I asked, 'Would you like to dance?' She answered . . . 'No.' My world fell apart. My life was over. Everything felt completely meaningless. Until six weeks later, that is, when I fell head over heels for Karoline. However, the same situation played out at the next school party. By the time I had singled five girls out as the objects of my affections and suffered five rejections, my brain had decided to create two false beliefs in order to protect me from this kind of psychological torment for the rest of my life. The first false belief was that girls are a source of pain that is best avoided. The second false belief was that I was ugly. These two beliefs maintained their grip on me until I turned thirty-five and learned that our brains create beliefs like this to automate our emotions and protect us from pain. These two false beliefs had definitely outstayed their welcome. Part of the process I went through to create a new version of myself involved listing all the 'beliefs' that I subscribed to that were holding me back, and addressing them. I'll give you the three best techniques I discovered for eliminating false beliefs below.

Re-Evaluate Your References

This was the technique I used to rid myself of the 'truth' 'I am ugly'. To do this, you'll need two sheets of paper. On one, write down the events and experiences that gave rise to your 'old truth'. In my case, I was able to write down four or five memories and reference points that had specifically contributed to generating the false belief that I was ugly. On the second sheet of paper, you write down situations that give evidence to the contrary. In my case, I wrote down all the times anyone had said anything positive about my appearance, or taken an interest in my inner or external 'attractiveness'. It turned out that there was quite a long list of evidence I had been ignoring. Placing these lists next to one another made it obvious what the real truth was, and my old self-image fell apart fairly quickly.

Apply a Different Standard

I used to live with the persistent notion that I wasn't a good leader. The problem wasn't that there was anything wrong with my leadership, but, rather, the false belief I held about what makes somebody a good leader. My idea was that a good leader is a loving leader, and that if you're not loving, you can't be a good leader. However, once I expanded my idea of what makes a good leader, I realized that people who possess a powerful drive and have strong visions can be just as effective as leaders. So, just by arriving at this new realization, I was able to eliminate my learned false belief. I had simply been applying the wrong standard. I was forty-four when I realized this, and I know it might sound strange but false beliefs can blind us, and once they have become automatic parts of us, we won't even notice that they're controlling us. The same might apply to women who don't feel feminine enough, or men who don't feel masculine enough – it all just comes down to whatever they've internalized as the 'belief' about what femininity or masculinity really are. By questioning where this belief actually came from, and finding alternative standards to apply, you can break free of old beliefs that are holding you back.

Make Up Your Mind

By deciding to see the false belief as the idiotic function it really is, you can topple and overcome it. It can really be that simple. That's precisely what happened to me when I overcame the 'belief' that I have a poor sense of direction. I realized that it had mostly come about as a result of having so many funny stories to tell about it. This false belief had created an entertaining persona I could adopt in social situations. The problem was that I didn't really have such a poor sense of direction. What actually tended to happen was that my brain was often too preoccupied with analysing and thinking about a bunch of stuff, and I would often forget to keep an eye out for signs. I decided to start keeping an eye out for signs, and, just like that, the problem was solved.

Tool 9: Conflicting Beliefs

A potential stressor in life is when beliefs appear to conflict – this is often referred to as cognitive dissonance. It can either be a case of an individual embracing two incompatible beliefs, or of an individual holding something to be true that conflicts with what their partner or the rest of the world holds to be true.

My first experience of holding two conflicting beliefs came just a few years ago. The first of these beliefs was formed when I was eighteen and made a list of rather superficial life goals for myself: Porsche at twenty-five, millionaire at thirty, live by the Mediterranean at some point and retire by forty-two. Over the course of my life, particularly after the age of thirty-five or so, a new belief had gradually taken root within me: I wanted to offer free communication training to all the children of the world. At forty-two, the conflict between these beliefs came to a head. I saw no way of combining these beliefs, and, believe it or not, this situation brought me a great deal of stress and fatigue. I actually think I've never experienced anything quite like it. The situation was resolved quite dramatically when I was in my home gym and experienced my first-ever fit of rage. I was angry with myself. I yelled, threw things, tore at my hair and ended up collapsing on my yoga mat, finally accepting that I would have to give up what had been my primary focus since I was eighteen – that I should retire by the age of forty-two. My new belief seemed far more important to the person I had become. The relief I experienced after this is perhaps best described as a triple Angel's cocktail that lasted for months.

If your belief happens to be that your children's rooms need to be neat and tidy, while your partner believes that this isn't really too important, you're holding conflicting beliefs. While neither one of you is right per se, the incompatibility of your convictions can definitely cause strain in your relationship. There are, essentially, three solutions to this problem if you want to enjoy a long-term relationship with the minimum of stress: 1) One of you will have to alter your belief. 2) You will have to choose to accept the difference. 3) You will have to accept the difference and choose to emphasize the positive aspects that your partner brings to the relationship and you don't, and focus on appreciating the balance you strike together.

If, for example, your belief happens to be that it's important to be environmentally minded, your belief will conflict with the behaviour of anybody who doesn't feel the same as you do or who isn't prepared to make the same effort you do. You could even want to be environmentally minded and experience cognitive dissonance by choosing to fly somewhere despite knowing that this is an unsustainable lifestyle choice in terms of the planet's resources. Depending on the strength of your belief, and the extent to which you're willing to defend it, conflicting beliefs can provide a lot of drive, as well as a lot of stress.

Tool 10: Dopamine vs Cortisol

In a study carried out by a team led by Martina Svensson at Lund University, a rat was allowed free use of an exercise wheel whenever it wanted to run. Another rat, on the other hand, was forced to run whenever the first rat chose to run. The stress levels of the second rat were significantly higher than those of the first rat, which was running of its own volition. What caused the difference? Dopamine is what makes an event feel enjoyable and positive, and this reduces our stress levels. The conclusion, then, is that it's of vital importance that you find genuine motivation in the things you do and the tasks you perform. If you fail to do this, you'll be in danger of cortisol and stress becoming your dominant driving force instead of dopamine.

Interestingly we can see the effects of this whenever this shift occurs in humans. They get to work, feeling incredibly motivated, and their dopamine flows freely. However, after a few years, they may begin to feel more stressed than motivated. Perhaps they've set overambitious goals for themselves, had a change of management or co-workers, or received new tasks that felt less motivating. Rather than feeling motivated and running on dopamine, they begin to feel stressed and run instead on cortisol, which means that they end up having to force themselves to complete their tasks. One consequence of having excessive cortisol levels for prolonged periods can be what is often called a 'beer belly' – an abdominal obesity that is produced by the accumulation of the blood sugar that has been released by the cortisol for so long, and ends up not being used the 'right' way, to activate and fuel muscles.

Tool 11: Break the Pattern

If somebody gives you negative criticism, it's not entirely unlikely that later on you'll find yourself repeating to yourself what they said. The more often you do this, the more convinced your brain will become that this is an important detail to remember and relevant to your survival. It will become a 'truth'. This will, in turn, cause your brain to carry on repeating this new belief to you, in an endless loop, to the point where you won't even notice it happening any more. Perhaps somebody told you, at some point or other, that you have a big nose, and you went on to repeat that to yourself. As a result, your brain determined that this was important information, and set about repeating it back to you with increasing frequency. The equation is simple: the more often you feed your brain a piece of information, the more likely it will start repeating it as a belief, without any conscious action on your part.

This is where the technique of breaking the pattern can be useful. The idea here is to prevent your thought loop from completing. Rather than 'I have an ugly nose; it's far too big and awkward-looking', you try to break your train of thought at 'I have . . .' You just don't allow the loop to repeat. This will signal to your brain that the thought is no longer as important, since you didn't even bother finishing it. As a result, it will come to be repeated less often going forward. When you receive criticism from somebody, you can use this technique to break the loop within the first few minutes or hours. However, if the loop has already had several years to ingrain itself in you, my experience tells me that it could take two to three weeks of consistent pattern breaking to disconnect it. My favourite techniques for breaking patterns are: word games, breathing exercises, listening to music, watching the sitcom *Seinfeld*, calling a friend, meditating, breathing, splashing my face with cold water, unexpected actions or motions, singing a song or focusing on external details, like counting and observing specific objects and colours in my surroundings.

This break-the-pattern technique isn't a very useful approach for preventing anxiety from spiralling out of control. In that situation, you're better off accepting your anxiety, and using relaxation and breathing exercises to quell your stress response. If you try to pattern-break anxiety, it can feel as though you're 'running' from it, and even make you feel worse. A study by Barnaby D. Dunn and others evaluated the technique by asking participants to look at the bloody effects of a car crash. The participants who were asked to break the pattern immediately after looking at the pictures and video clips, and to get their brains to think of something other than the crash, were less emotionally impacted and less able to recall the details of the pictures and videos than those who didn't break the pattern and instead allowed themselves to carry on internally repeating their experiences of seeing the pictures.

To sum this section up: if you receive negative criticism, listen to it, learn from it, but break the pattern. If you see something you don't want to remember, break the pattern.

Dial Up Your Stress

Stress can be a wonderful thing in small doses, so I thought that now we'd do something rather unexpected: learn to dial up your stress. Why would you ever want to do that? During that summer I spent crying in my bed, I took blood tests that revealed that my cortisol levels were extremely low. This was why I felt so drained. It became essential for me to raise my cortisol, and I managed to do so by combining use of the stress map with daily meditation. About six months later, my levels were back to normal, and my energy had recovered.

I trigger a stress response deliberately whenever I'm about to give a lecture and when, for whatever reason, I feel that my motivation is lacking. When this happens, I can easily choose to simulate fear by pretending that I'm being hunted by something. Let's try this simple exercise together! You'll probably notice your energy levels increase as a result of the cortisol release, feel a tingling sensation in your body caused by adrenaline and experience a heightened sense of focus thanks to the noradrenaline. I should, however, warn you not to try this exercise if you suffer from anxiety, as rapid hyperventilation can trigger anxiety attacks. Stop immediately if it makes you feel disoriented or uncomfortable in any way.

Here's how to perform the exercise. Take between five to twenty seconds for each stage:

1. Sit down.
2. Imagine that you're being hunted.
3. Move your head and eyes about in rapid, jerky motions.
4. Tense every muscle in your body.
5. Look around the room, and behind you, as if you were being hunted by something.
6. Start taking quick, forceful breaths.

As a bonus, after finishing this exercise, try taking seven breaths a minute by doing the slow-breathing technique we went over earlier. This will allow you to experience an exciting and fascinating contrast!

Cortisol — A Summary

Stress is amazing! It's healthy in small, brief doses, so you should make a point of enjoying it every day by introducing new activities, seeking out excitement, venturing beyond your comfort zone, challenging your problems and learning along the way. However, large doses of stress, lasting for prolonged periods of time, will cause you harm. If that's what your life is like, you should use the stress map, break your patterns, meditate, engage in low-intensity exercise, look over your accepted beliefs and apply as much as you can from the chapter on oxytocin (page 51), because oxytocin provides powerful stress relief.

Endorphins

Euphoria

Welcome to the euphoric side of life: endorphins! The term has an interesting origin; it is composed of the words 'endogenous', which refers to substances originating within the body, and 'morphine', which is an opiate named after the Greek god of dreams, Morpheus. Endorphins, then, are the body's home-grown morphine. The big difference between endorphins and medical morphine is that you can create them for yourself and that they're not solely used for pain relief. They make a great addition to an Angel's cocktail when you want to feel 'high on life'.

Tool 1: Choose Your Pain

How can you release endorphins at will? It's really quite easy to do, and there are several ways you can do it – although some are more pleasant than others! Let's begin with a practical example that will also give us a good reference point for discussing the subjective experience of endorphins. Have you ever rushed between two rooms, and somehow forgotten that doorways tend to have thresholds? Have you ever stubbed your big toe on one with incredible force? The pain that follows is usually horrendous. However, few of us take the opportunity to enjoy the endorphin high that usually arrives ten seconds or so later. Personally I make a point of doing this in situations like that. Whenever I stub my toe or bump some other part of my body, I lie down on the floor on my back, breathe calmly and stare up at the ceiling while counting to ten. After this, I'm filled with a near-euphoric feeling that's caused by the endorphins that are pouring into my body. This feeling lasts for about a minute, and if you pay attention, you'll notice that you tend to go from euphoric to relieved to practically painless – unless you broke something, of course.

I remember very clearly how one day, a long time ago, Maria came to me complaining about how she was in such pain. 'What happened?' I asked her.

'I don't know. I went to the gym two days ago, and I might be in pain because of that.'

I slowly turned to face her, and said, 'You mean you're experiencing delayed-onset muscle soreness? It's completely normal to feel sore after working out. The soreness is just proof that you did well at the gym.'

She looked somewhat hesitant, nodded and said OK. A month or so later, she came bouncing into the kitchen to announce, 'I'm sore from working out, and it feels great!'

Paradoxically, pain can be pleasurable. Take my love of cold-water bathing, for example. I do have to count out thirty seconds before I can feel the endorphins kicking in, but, my goodness, when they do it's an incredible feeling!

I doubt I'll ever forget the first time I laid down on a bed of nails. I went from paralysing fear to absolute euphoria in an instant. While I can't say for sure if this was caused by endorphins, the experience was extremely similar. If I hadn't chosen to view the pain as a positive that time, I would never have climbed on to that bed of nails, and I would never have experienced what I did.

Occasionally I have had to take blood tests and the needle can sometimes hurt going in. It makes quite an astonishing difference whether I choose to focus on this pain from a negative place, such as fear, or from a positive place, by, say, thinking about how wonderful modern healthcare is, and how grateful I am to be able to just go and take a blood test like this.

I'd like to close by telling you about one of the craziest ideas I've had in some time: deliberately growing brown adipose tissue by exposing myself to cold. Brown adipose tissue can be thought of as a little furnace in the body, a source of heat inside you that can light up when you get cold. It also offers some quite powerful health benefits. What I did was launch the Nordic January T-Shirt Challenge, which was open to anyone who wanted to participate. The challenge was to wear nothing but a T-shirt on your upper body throughout the month of January (no exceptions!). I got so cold! I spent the first two weeks shivering non-stop, day and night. It was torturous, but it was also incredibly fascinating. I made two exciting observations. First, I felt extremely energized after my morning walks, while my friends, who were wrapped up to keep the cold away, tended to feel fatigued afterwards. Second, it took about two and a half weeks for me to stop feeling freezing, after which I began to find it quite uncomfortable to wear a lot of clothes. Perhaps this was proof that I had actually managed to put on some brown adipose tissue. I chose to suffer the pain of freezing in order to gain the positive health benefits of brown adipose tissue, which include preventing obesity, diabetes, insulin resistance and cancer growth, as well as a number of cardiovascular benefits. However, it also has the added benefit of stopping you from freezing all the time. How did the other participants do? Well, half of them made it all the way to the finishing line, and they all looked pretty proud.

Many people I meet have chosen to avoid pain that could actually be constructive, like temporary exposure to the cold, temporary hunger and physical exercise. If these individuals were to challenge their pain instead, and approach it head-on, they would be giving themselves an opportunity to grow and feel a whole lot better.

Tool 2: Smile

Apart from endorphins, smiling also produces serotonin and dopamine. It seems obvious, therefore, that smiling makes us feel good. But does that mean we're able to smile on command, and do we reap the same benefits from this? A large meta-study, which compiled data from 138 studies involving a total of 11,000 respondents, determined that test subjects felt happier when they smiled, regardless of whether they did so on command as part of an experiment or spontaneously. I read about these results, but then it struck me that I wasn't able to smile – at least not genuinely. A 'genuine' smile is a concept defined by and named after the neurologist Guillaume Duchenne. He determined that a genuine smile occurs when both the muscles of the eyes (the *orbicularis oculi*) and the muscles that run along the cheekbone to the corner of the mouth (*musculus zygomaticus major*) are contracted in coordination.

The benefits of a Duchenne smile are quite significant. What would you say if somebody told you there was a way for you to be perceived as more credible, become less likely to be divorced, become more likely to be married, become happier and live longer just by smiling a certain way? Naturally I wanted to be able to do this. I went straight to our Google Photos archive, which has 60,000 pictures of our family and 5,000 pictures of me. I browsed through the pictures for ages, but I couldn't find any pictures of me wearing a genuine smile. This isn't too remarkable, I suppose, considering how depressed I have felt for most of my adult life. On the other hand, I did find pictures of me smiling that way from when I was a child. I suppose I had simply forgotten how it was done.

As always when I want to learn something new, I dedicated myself fully to this cause. I practised and practised, and people in the neighbourhood must have suspected that I was a massive psychopath for a while there. But try as I might, I couldn't get it right. I needed some kind of reference – I needed to experience that smile first-hand. I thought about what made me the happiest, and thus the most likely to flash a proper Duchenne smile. Soon I determined that this was probably when I would return home from a few weeks on the road, and regardless of the weather, my daughter would run out to meet me by the car in her socks, press her head against my neck and tell me she missed me. If I didn't have a Duchenne smile when that happened, I didn't think there was any hope for me. So I devised a plan: I would make a point of trying to feel whether that smile came over me in that moment when my daughter hugged me the next time I came home. A few weeks later, it happened. I rolled up the driveway in my car, and saw the front door fly open. Leona ran out to me in her socks, ready to throw her arms and legs around me, and, as usual, she pressed her head against my neck. And, bless my analytical approach, there it was! I felt my face behave in a way I wasn't accustomed to. As soon as we got inside, I went to the bathroom to look at myself in the mirror, to examine my smile. It was glorious. After this, I started practising. I had a memory now, a muscular point of reference, and I had proof that I was capable of producing that smile. A few months later, genuine smiles felt completely natural to me. In other words, I can produce a Duchenne smile at will, whenever I want to. This is particularly effective when I get nervous during a presentation, a meeting or a lecture. Flashing a quick Duchenne smile is a great way to soothe my nerves. Those situations make it incredibly clear to me how smiles can relieve pain by releasing endorphins. Perhaps this is also why we so often try to smile when we become anxious, or laugh when we're afraid.

Tool 3: Laughter

Laughing is an extension of smiling, of course, but unlike smiling it has the potential to produce a more powerful euphoric effect, like the one you can get after stubbing your toe. Consider a genuine belly laugh, the kind that makes you feel cramp develop in your abdominal muscles. When that kind of laughter ends, you'll usually feel a bit high and euphoric. It's the activation of the abdominal muscles that helps laughter trigger such a huge amount of endorphins compared to smiling. That's why laughter yoga, which is largely based on laughing from your abdomen, is a thing. Interestingly it's been found that the more opioid receptors you have in your brain, the more you'll tend to laugh at something funny. Good for you!

The endorphin family includes alpha-endorphins, gamma-endorphins and beta-endorphins. The latter have been highlighted in a large number of studies exploring social relationships and situations such as being touched by a romantic partner, participating in synchronized group activities and feeling a sense of connectedness. One theory is that this might be a reward system related to the social situations in question. The effects of these beta-endorphins are exciting too, as they have been proven to boost our ability to interpret the emotions of others and empathize with their situation. It's no surprise really that most of our smiling happens in social situations. Professor Sophie Scott has found that we are 30 per cent more likely to laugh during social encounters than we are when we're on our own.

Laughter isn't even necessarily a response to something funny – it's often used more as a kind of social signal. Laughing and smiling don't just make us feel good; they've also proven to be great social-bonding agents. Unfortunately there are many people out there who are the way I used to be, i.e. people who very rarely smile or laugh. You might be one of them, but if you are, at least you know now that it's just a matter of practice.

Tool 4: Spicy Food

Now, if pain produces endorphins, it's not too far-fetched to suggest that painful sensations in your mouth might do the same thing. Spicy food is often said to be addictive, and while endorphins certainly aren't addictive, it's quite clear to me what's going on here.

Tool 5: Exercise

Exercise produces endorphins, but since exercise has so many other beneficial effects, I've chosen to discuss it in the chapter on page 171.

Tool 6: Music

Several studies, including one by T. Najafi Ghezeljeh from Iran University of Medical Sciences, suggest that music can provide mild pain relief by producing endorphins that raise people's pain thresholds. In some parts of the world, music is actively used as an analgesic. Perhaps there is a certain kind of music that you often listen to when you feel the need to soothe emotional pain. This was definitely something I realized about myself when I learned about this connection.

Tool 7: Chocolate

Chocolate lovers, rejoice! In her 2017 study, Dr Thea Magrone demonstrated that all we need to do to enjoy the euphoric effects of endorphins is gorge ourselves on chocolate. Dopamine levels have also been shown to rise by 150 per cent when we eat chocolate, so it offers a proper double whammy of benefits. Although, compared to the euphoria I get from stubbing my toe, I can't claim that the endorphins I get from eating chocolate are really that intense.

Tool 8: Dancing

I spent about 400 of the 700 days of the lockdown phase of the Covid-19 pandemic standing in front of a camera, delivering lectures from my manor's conference centre, rather than travelling around to do so as I was used to. It was quite challenging for me to get pumped up for all these lectures at first, but we soon developed our methods. I asked my cameraman to switch on the disco lights we had installed, turn on the smoke machine and blast out an Avicii song, and then I pulled shapes, all by myself, for three minutes or so. This had an incredible effect on my mood, excitement and happiness. This is really no wonder, though, when you consider all the endorphins that are released when we dance. Dancing with others helps raise your pain threshold and forms a stronger social bond with the people you dance with – two effects that are very probably connected to the endorphins involved. I'd like to add here that dancing also brings a lot of other benefits besides the endorphins. When you feel the need for a mood-lifting cocktail, it's always a good idea to dance, especially when you have company.

Tool 9: Cold Exposure

Most people who take cold-water baths do it the 'wrong' way, at least if you ask me. Perhaps it would be fairer of me to say that most people could better optimize, enjoy and benefit from the practice. Here is the formula I use, which it has taken me a thousand or so cold-water baths to arrive at. It's important to state that I can't take responsibility for the effects a cold-water bath might have on you, and I advise you to do it in the company of a friend, preferably in shallow waters. If you know that you're prone to anxiety attacks, I would also advise that you have professional help at hand, as the experience can trigger anxiety. However, for most of us, a cold-water bath brings nothing but pure euphoria.

My Formula for the Optimal Cold-Water Bath

Enter the cold water immediately, and make sure that your shoulders are submerged – this is important! The instant effect will be that your sympathetic nervous system will respond to the pain and the perceived danger, and cause you to tense up and start to hyperventilate. Most inexperienced cold-water bathers make a frantic escape from the water at this point, and if they happen to be in a spa, this no doubt fetches a mixture of looks of admiration and judgement from the group in the hot tub a few metres away. But don't get out of the water!

Instead, breathe in through your nose and exhale through your mouth, as slowly as you possibly can. As soon as you've gained control of your breathing, move on to deliberately relaxing your muscles. Both these activities (calm breathing and muscle relaxation) will help you control your immediate stress response (which is regulated by your sympathetic nervous system). You're about fifteen seconds in now. Wait for another fifteen seconds, and then dip your face into the water. Doing this will activate the diving reflex, which is innate in all humans. This will bring your heart rate down and help your breathing relax further. By this point, thirty seconds should have gone by. It's around this time that you can expect to start experiencing the pain-relieving and euphoric effects of endorphins. This is also the stage when you'll usually need to give yourself another reminder to relax your muscles. After about forty-five seconds, you should be free to fully enjoy the experience. Move your focus out of yourself and your bodily sensations, and just let go and take in the beauty of the world. If you're outdoors, listen to the birds. If you're in the shower, enjoy the colours and patterns of the tiling. Do this for another fifteen to thirty seconds, and then get out of the water and celebrate your accomplishment!

Once you're out, take another moment to enjoy all the reactions that are going on in your body, and make sure to appreciate all the beauty that surrounds you. You'll be feeling the effects of a massive cocktail of endorphins, noradrenaline and dopamine – and although nobody has proven it yet, I think serotonin is also an obvious component of the glorious satisfaction and pride this activity produces. Congratulations! You've just transitioned from panic to euphoria in sixty seconds – an emotional journey that's incredibly difficult to make that quickly in any other way. The effects usually last for hours afterwards. During all my classes in self-leadership, whatever the time of year happens to be, the participants are given the opportunity to try cold-water bathing. I've coached many people through this experience, and I've found that even those who have suffered anxiety attacks have been able to learn to cope with them if they have the benefit of receiving coaching in real time. It gives them an incredibly clear and potent demonstration of how powerful it can be to control your breathing and dare to go along with your pain rather than run from it.

Endorphins – A Summary

Like the cherry on top or a slice of lime, endorphins make a great garnish for your Angel's cocktail. I love to smile and laugh, and it feels rather strange to me now that there was a time when I didn't do these things. If you feel that you're not smiling or laughing as much as you'd like to, I implore you to learn to do it, for your own sake! Maximize your Angel's cocktail by allowing yourself to smile and laugh more, and sprinkling hundreds of little doses of endorphins on top of your day. Why not start out with a dance number, a good run or a lovely cold-water bath, and give your sense of euphoria a proper endorphin boost?

Testosterone

Confidence and Wins

Welcome to the wonderful world of testosterone! This is the sixth and final substance that we'll be discussing from the point of view of how you can benefit from adding it to your Angel's cocktail. The biggest source of confusion in regard to testosterone is the common idea that it is related to aggressive behaviour, but as you'll soon learn, that's far from always the case.

The key to understanding how this actually works lies with the testosterone itself. Dr Robert Sapolsky likes to describe the primary effect of testosterone as one of amplification. Testosterone amplifies the tools you already use to improve your social status. In other words, your serotonin levels reflect your current social status, and your testosterone provides you with the tools for improving it. One potential tool for achieving improved social status is violence, and in this regard testosterone can make you more aggressive. However, if your tool of choice for improving your social status happens to be generosity, testosterone will amplify that behaviour instead. If your tool for improving your social status is your sense of humour, testosterone will make you funnier. If you usually try to come up with new inventions or ideas to improve your social status, testosterone will amplify your creativity. Sapolsky has even joked about this in an interview: 'It's probably even the case that if you stoked up some Buddhist monks with tons of testosterone, they'd become wildly competitive as to who can do the most acts of random kindness.' Testosterone, then, is an extremely powerful substance, which serves to amplify behaviours that you already exhibit.

It's worth noting before we continue that both men and women possess the sex hormone testosterone, and the same is true of oestrogen. Men tend to have more testosterone than women, while women tend to have more oestrogen than men. The psychological effects of an identical increase in testosterone, however, are usually similar in both men and women. An exciting conclusion I've drawn after all the self-leadership courses I've given is that the female participants enjoy the testosterone exercises the most and also express a greater perceived difference. Perhaps this is because they don't usually have as many opportunities to experience rapid testosterone boosts.

When I learned about how testosterone impacts our social status, it made me pause and consider which learned behaviours I tended to use to elevate my social status. I soon determined that I didn't fit neatly into any of the more common pigeonholes: I didn't use expensive, fancy belongings as a means of gaining social status, nor did I rely on seeking social status by association through activities like name-dropping. Instead, my behaviour in this regard seemed to depend more on five other factors: 1) My core skill set, which involves communication skills used on stage or in a room. I realized that I enjoy using these abilities to improve my own social status. 2) Sharing knowledge.

3) Helping others. 4) Being inventive and creative. 5) Being different. These points aren't presented in any kind of hierarchical order here. Their importance to me varies depending on the time and situation in question. Why don't you take some time to consider what your own approaches tend to be? Put the book down, lean back and consider which of your social behaviours you usually emphasize when your social status comes under threat or when you simply want to strengthen it. Here are some tips that might help you figure this out: think of how you behave in social situations in which you're completely new, what you post on social media and what you do at work or school when you want to receive more attention and recognition. The properties I listed were all positive ones, but aggression can also be used as a means for elevating social status. Other negative methods I've observed include putting people down, belittling them, badmouthing them, exaggerating, playing the victim, insisting on always being right and sub-tler approaches, including raising your voice, using superior language or displaying superior body language.

An interesting reflection on our need to turn up the volume to acquire social influence is that practically every-body does this. And if practically everybody is doing it, this means you can also learn by being observant of how the people around you behave. Do they go about gaining status in positive or negative ways? If you practise this, you can learn to better understand when somebody is feeling socially disadvantaged and help them as the situation requires. Per-haps using testosterone allows us to rise within the social hierarchy, which is one of the ways we can affect somebody's serotonin levels, but this elevated status will, in turn, also bring about the other effect of serotonin, which is a positive outlook and a sense of increased well-being.

Testosterone also plays a role in risk-taking. That is to say, higher levels of testosterone can make us more willing to accept risks. However, there is an ongoing debate regarding the role testosterone plays in this, and it seems that other factors might also be part of the equation. A fairly recent hypothesis suggests that what really promotes risk-taking could be cortisol and testosterone in combination. In a review of the literature carried out by Jennifer Kurath and Rui Mata, a correlation, albeit rather weak, was discovered.

A third exciting effect of testosterone is that it can help boost our confidence. Testosterone is connected to competitiveness, and makes us less disposed to give up, according to Hana Kutlikova of the University of Vienna. Another researcher, Colin Camerer, has shown how testosterone can weaken our impulse control, which can also be interpreted as a case of increased confidence. Our society values confidence very highly, and it has probably also played an important role in our evolution. Human beings are generally uncomfortable with uncertainty, and most of us prefer security over insecurity. A confident leader, salesperson, potential mate, negotiator or presenter will generally seem more attractive than a less-confident alternative.

During my self-leadership course, I guide participants through experiences involving each of the substances addressed in this book, and this includes an exploration of the sensations related to testosterone. The descriptions my participants give of experiencing testosterone differ quite starkly from the ones they give for the other five substances. Words that often appear are 'invincible', 'strong', 'cocky', 'powerful' and 'fearless', and, as I mentioned earlier, women tend to feel the effects more strongly than men.

Being able to raise your testosterone deliberately, at will, which for practical purposes means being able to boost your confidence on command, is quite the little super-power. So let's move on to discussing ways you can do that.

Tool 1: Wins

Victories, or wins, boost our testosterone levels. What constitutes a win, however, is very subjective. Somebody who wins the New York Marathon could still be disappointed with their performance if they fail to complete the race faster than the last time they ran it. This person will thus gain less testosterone than somebody who ends up in seventeenth place but beat their personal best by five minutes and was so exhausted during the race that they worried they would have to withdraw.

Whenever I'm about to give a digital lecture from the JP Manor, and I'm feeling a little lacklustre or downtrodden, or I feel that the lecture isn't going to go well, I ask my team to take a fifteen-minute break beforehand so we can engage in some competitive activity. Usually this means a Nerf session is about to begin. Nerf guns are plastic weapons that fire foam darts, and we enjoy chasing each other around the manor with them. Everybody gets pretty into it, and we usually have a lot of fun. So we spend fifteen minutes fighting for our lives with Nerf guns, and, sure enough, I feel my testosterone increase as we play. Before I know it, I feel more than ready to give my very best performance.

Other ways of producing a similar feeling could be playing a game you feel quite confident you'll win, or challenging somebody to a contest you reckon you're better at. Unless my slump is particularly severe, I can usually give myself a reliable boost just by thinking back to past wins and successes.

Researcher P. C. Bernhardt wanted to investigate whether football fans experience testosterone boosts similar to the ones that previous studies had established that players on the pitch experience. The results showed that fans of the winning team can show 20 per cent increases in their testosterone levels, while the levels of the fans of the losing team can decrease by the same amount. All in all, that means there can be a 40 per cent difference between the fans of the winning team and the fans of the losing team.

Interestingly the levels of the football players themselves tended to rise regardless of whether they won or lost. According to a study by researchers at Berkeley University in California, USA, football players can experience an immediate spike of 30 per cent when they play, and still be 15 per cent above their baseline the next day. Benjamin Trumble, who co-authored the study, made the comment that, although the study was conducted on men, he expected that results would be similar for women.

Tool 2: Music

According to a study conducted by a team led by Hirokazu Doi of Nagasaki University, men who have higher levels of testosterone tend not to appreciate 'complicated' music, such as jazz or classical music. On the other hand, they do tend to like rock music. I think most of us are familiar with the impulse to drive a little faster when a certain kind of music comes on in the car. It's the same at the gym: listening to certain kinds of music can make you feel physically stronger and more 'badass'. Other research has shown that music tends to raise testosterone levels in both men and women. This offers us some exciting potential for dual benefits, as the music you listen to at the gym can also be used to access the feeling you had there in other situations.

Tool 3: Control Your Body

As an expert in presentation skills, I've spent years studying thousands of lecturers, and even defined and catalogued 110 body and voice techniques we can all use to improve our communication. (If you haven't yet seen it, check out my TEDx talk 'The 110 Techniques of Communication and Public Speaking'.) Thanks to all this experience, I can easily spot every technique that somebody is using incorrectly to boost their own confidence. I also know that minor adjustments to their use of those techniques can help them get things just right, and make them feel a lot more confident.

I have particularly strong memories of one person I coached. His facial features and body type immediately qualified him as an incredibly handsome man. On top of this, he was dressed like a fashion model and had the hair of a Greek god. He was an absolute ten. He entered the room with long, deliberate strides, a steely gaze and a strong firm handshake that he underlined with a confident smile. We spoke briefly and then I asked him to do a run-through of his presentation. After connecting his computer and going over to stand in the corner, he got started. Almost immediately he fell apart in front of my eyes. There are seven common physical signs that indicate low confidence: a swaying body, twisting hips, a downcast gaze, unparallel feet, arms locked in front of the body, filler sounds and a low voice. This man ticked all seven boxes. I was shocked.

I had never seen a transformation like the one I had just witnessed. Nobody had ever just crumpled like that in my presence. I described to him exactly what I had seen, and, as you might expect, I soon learned that he had had some rather deflating experiences giving presentations at work in the past, and had responded to these by creating the false truth for himself that he was a bad presenter. We started working on the seven factors in turn, and when he seemed to be ready, I asked him to do another run-through of his presentation. Afterwards, when I showed him video recordings of his first and second attempts, he burst into tears. He told me he had never imagined that the difference could be this huge, and that this went way beyond just the body language; he felt that he could actually see his true self-image shine now when he spoke. He also found it incredible that we had achieved such a massive change in so short an amount of time. Problem solved. He went on practising body language that signalled to his brain that 'everything is cool, I own this', and the effect stuck with him. He started racking up wins giving presentations, and soon he was every bit as dominant a presence on stage as he was in the other areas of his life. While this is one of my more extreme examples, I have plenty of other cases I could mention where a small change in body language or voice had an immediate impact on somebody's confidence. I can't say for sure that these effects were caused by testosterone, because I didn't measure his testosterone levels before or after the change, but I feel confident enough all the same to say that his testosterone was almost certainly higher afterwards.

When you want to boost your confidence before doing something, you should remember to hold your head up high, plant your feet parallel to each other, use your hands rather than allowing them to lock up, avoid swaying or twisting your hips, train yourself to eliminate filler noises from your speech, and speak up loud and clear. To summarize: stand and move as though you ruled the world ten minutes before any activity that you feel the need to boost your confidence for. Feel free to combine this technique with music and the visualizations we discussed earlier for an even more powerful effect.

Tool 4: Confidence

After my meeting with the 'male model' who went from confident to human wreck and then back again so quickly, I became even more impressed by how much we can influence our own confidence levels. Confidence has a lot to do with the activities we're engaging in. For example, somebody might start playing basketball, and as they rack up an increasing number of wins, their confidence and sense of security in playing basketball will grow. However, this won't have much of an effect on their confidence in presenting juggling tricks or entering a political debate. But if our basketball player were to go on that same journey playing volleyball and football, and develop their confidence in relation to those sports, they would probably be more confident if they decided to give hockey a try one day. It's important that you realize this in relation to your own confidence. Confidence isn't some static thing. Rather, it's a dynamic state that we can develop in different areas of our lives and cultivate through practice and the accumulation of successes.

Tool 5: Introversion vs Extroversion

Inside your brain there is an area that consists of a cluster of something called raphe nuclei. Here there is a small constellation of dopamine neurons that perform various functions, including producing a desire in you for social interactions.

When your social appetite is sated, the dopamine will be released. The difference between an introvert and an extrovert is that an extrovert will have a greater appetite for social interactions. In other words, they'll need to spend longer in social activities to feel socially sated than introverts.

One of the most revealing studies on this subject, which was conducted by Maureen M. J. Smeets-Janssen, showed that extroverted individuals tend to have more testosterone. Are introversion and extroversion static states? Not at all. They can vary depending on the dynamics of a situation and the way somebody feels on a certain day. I've been rather introverted for most of my life, but since recovering from my depression, I've gradually become increasingly extroverted. My social hunger takes longer to satisfy these days. Just as you can practise playing basketball and thus become more confident in basketball-related situations, you can practise social interactions and become more confident in social situations.

Tool 6: Movies

It probably won't come as a surprise to you that watching a movie is an activity that has the potential to boost our testosterone levels. For this to happen, it's important that we're able to relate to the protagonist, and that we can empathize with them and feel that we're somehow involved in their successes. One study showed that men's testosterone levels were raised by watching Don Corleone in *The Godfather*, while women's levels dropped. However, they maintained their levels of testosterone while watching *Bridget Jones's Diary*, while men's levels tended to drop. As we learned earlier from the football study, we need to feel a very strong level of commitment to a team in order to experience a testosterone boost if they win. Similarly we need to strongly identify with a character in a film for the same effect to occur.

Tool 7: Aggression

According to Dr Robert Sapolsky, whom we met earlier, aggression causes testosterone levels to rise. One trick for using aggression to raise your testosterone can be to go to the bathroom before an important meeting and think aggressive thoughts, ideally complementing this with menacing body language and intense music. If nobody will hear me, I'll often yell aggressively while doing this too, in order to maximize the temporary aggression and boost my testosterone even more.

In this context, however, I feel I should mention that uncontrolled aggression is a huge problem in our society, and that if you feel that your aggression tends to intensify as a result of feeling that your social status is being threatened, it's probably wisest for you to avoid triggering yourself unnecessarily. Instead, you should practise catching the signs, and learn to halt your aggression in time. Meditation works well for this. If you should find yourself experiencing this kind of aggression, try to breathe your way through it rather than acting out.

Testosterone — A Summary

Testosterone is an amazing ingredient in your Angel's cocktail that can be used to improve your performance in a variety of situations, including job interviews, social situations, negotiations and presentations. It's worth bearing in mind, however, that testosterone can potentially cloud your judgement and impair your impulse control. Don't forget this, and don't let a sudden rush of testosterone impact important decisions in your life.

You can also use testosterone to improve your confidence in the longer term by making a habit of listening to music that pumps you up, helps you move confidently or recalls past successes. Take risks when you might benefit from doing so. Train yourself to think of your setbacks and failures as fuel for future successes, and make sure to give yourself little wins in any area in which you'd like to feel more confident.

The Base of Your Angel's Cocktail

Becoming the best possible version of yourself requires good self-leadership, i.e. the ability to regulate your thoughts and decisions. There are many compromises you can make that won't stop you from achieving good self-leadership; however, there are four areas that you simply can't neglect if you want to succeed: sleep, diet, exercise and meditation. All these are so essential to your well-being that I could write entire books about each of them. The base you need to mix up a good Angel's cocktail can be summed up as: good sleep, a good diet, regular exercise and daily meditation. Here are my best recommendations for these areas.

Sleep

1. I belong to the absolute majority of grown-ups who need an average of seven to eight hours of sleep each night. Some people can get by on just six hours. The group of people who are medically able to sustain themselves on less sleep than this is extremely small, although the group of people who mistakenly believe they belong to it is rather large.

2. Deep sleep is one of the most important of the four sleep stages. An adult needs to spend 13–23 per cent of their night in a state of deep sleep to feel rested the next day. Deep sleep plays an important role in the processing of our memories. You can measure your deep sleep quite reliably using some smartwatches and activity trackers. These measurements will be more accurate if you sleep alone, as opposed to sharing your bed with your partner or child.

3. There are a few tricks you can use to make it easier for you to fall asleep and improve your sleep overall:

- Avoid the blue glare of screens during the last few hours before you go to bed.
- Keep your bedroom cool rather than warm.
- Make sure your bedroom is well ventilated, so carbon dioxide doesn't accumulate in there during the night. When you wake up, a carbon dioxide meter should indicate a lower concentration than 1,000 ppm; you want 600–700 ideally. These meters are available from most electronics shops.
- Sleep by yourself if others disturb your sleep at night.
- Go to bed when you feel tired (if you toss and turn in bed for more than half an hour, you aren't tired enough). To ensure you'll be tired

in the evening, you can do things that will mentally and physically tire you out during the day.

- Your twenty-four-hour clock, or circadian rhythm, is like an internal timer that gets you started in the morning by feeding you a burst of cortisol and other substances, and makes you feel sleepy at night by activating the secretion of melatonin. Now, this isn't the kind of timer you can set by turning a knob – the only way to set it is by taking sunlight in through your eyes. In the spring, autumn and winter, then, it's essential for you to absorb as much sun as possible in the mornings. It's a good idea to take a morning walk and look up at the light (although not directly at the sun). Watching the sun set has also been shown to have positive effects on setting the circadian rhythm.

- Avoid going to bed anxious – try to resolve any anxiety you may be experiencing before you go to bed. If you need to, meditate to gain a sense of inner calm.

- Alcohol has a negative impact on your quality of sleep, although it can sometimes seem to help.

- Let's close with the most important trick of all: go to bed at more or less the same time each night. This will help you establish a positive cycle of sleep and wakefulness.

Diet

1. Eating a varied diet will benefit your gut health and help you get enough of the important vitamins, minerals and trace elements. You should be eating fruits and greens, of course. I try to stick to a Mediterranean diet, as it has proven conducive to a long healthy life. It mainly consists of vegetables, fruit, fish, light meats, pulses, wholegrain products and healthy fats from sources like olive oil, nuts and seeds. I also limit my intake of red and processed meats, animal fats and food items that contain added sugars.

2. I minimize fast carbohydrates in order to avoid energy dips and the dopamine crashes that go along with them. Crashing like that makes you crave even more fast carbohydrates and makes you feel even more fatigued. It's better to prioritize slow carbohydrates over fast ones.

3. Don't forget to eat insoluble fibre, which you can get from wholegrain flour, nuts and beans. These foods will make you feel fuller and lower your risk of developing colonic or rectal cancer.

4. Avoid products that contain added refined sugar – they cause too many negative effects for me to list in this book.

5. I'm not much of a believer in legal nootropics, i.e. substances that supposedly enhance mental

capacity, like caffeine, L-theanine or modafinil.
You can achieve similar – and more long-lasting –
effects by ensuring you get good sleep, exercise,
food, social interactions and stress relief. You
already have an entire chemical plant in your
body that can mix you up any Angel's cocktail
you'd like! If you can learn to understand it and
put it to proper use, you'll be able to experience
the effects you want for the rest of your life.
However, if you rely on external substances like
coffee, cigarettes or pills to achieve the same
effects, you'll only be able to get those effects
when you have access to these crutches. I realize
this might seem a little extreme. I see the point,
for example, of using external substances to
learn how the effects you want to experience feel,
and then attempting to achieve the same effects
using self-leadership techniques. As always,
consult your doctor when consuming external
substances, especially if you are on any kind of
medication.

6. Minimize consumption of processed foods like
   ham, bacon and pâté, as there are proven links
   between those foods and conditions such as
   heart disease, type 2 diabetes and certain kinds of
   cancer.

7. Fish oil can be very helpful for preventing
   inflammation, according to a study conducted
   by a team at Tufts University in Boston, under
   the leadership of Jisun So. The fish oil that

proved to be the most potent anti-inflammatory was the kind that has a high content of the DHA omega-3 fatty acid – an ideal dose is upwards of a gram. The effects of fish oil on depression have been studied, and the results suggest that fish oil can positively affect our moods. However, if you're currently being treated for depression, you should always consult a doctor before adding fish oil or other supplements to your diet.

Exercise

Do you remember the description I gave of the inflammatory process on page 114 in the chapter on cortisol? I explained how cytokines, which are released during inflammation, influence our immune cells to gather the building block tryptophan (yep, the same one that's used for serotonin), and then use the enzyme Indoleamine 2,3-dioxygenase (IDO) to convert it into a substance called kynurenine, which is potentially neurotoxic. In slightly simplified terms, this means that long-term inflammation has two negative effects on our psychology. On the one hand, it depletes our access to the building blocks used to create serotonin, and on the other, it produces a substance that can poison our brains. The connection between this and exercise is that exercise helps your body process kynurenine, which in turn helps protect the brain from it, as discovered by Niklas Joisten at the German Sport University Cologne. Magic! Or, rather, biology!

I've maintained an exercise routine since I was eighteen and have only taken two long breaks from it. Both those breaks came as a result of some pretty extreme exercise projects. The first one was inspired by the film *Thor*, in which the shirtless Chris Hemsworth was, admittedly, quite an impressive sight. But what kick-started my motivation was really the sound I heard from right next to me. I heard Maria sort of slurp back a string of saliva when Hemsworth first came into view in his role as Thor. This inspired me to try to attain the physique of a Norse god, and for some reason I set my heart on doing this within six months. So I did what I always do and went for it 100 per cent. I hired a full-time personal trainer, asked a body-builder with several championships under his belt to design a special training programme for me, consulted with a nutritionist and began training harder than ever before. In six months I managed to put on nine kilograms of body weight, of which four were solid muscle mass. I was bursting shirts and my buttons were flying off during meetings – I ended up needing a whole new wardrobe. I reached my goal and I was delighted with my progress, but towards the end of the process I had been feeding myself far too much cortisol and nowhere near enough dopamine. I got through the last two months of the programme thanks to sheer willpower. As a result, I ended up losing all interest in exercise afterwards, and didn't pick it up again for a whole year.

During my life, I've tried countless training plans, but in the end I arrived at the only one that seems to be sustainable for me in the long term, which is to integrate exercise into my lifestyle. I train six days a week because it's a part of my life. I make sure to go for a long walk or go to the gym daily. I don't go hard; I go consistently. Our ancestors walked for miles and miles every day, and they definitely lifted more weight in a day than many of us do in a month. Our bodies were made to move.

Meditation

When I broke free from my recurring dark thoughts, I made two discoveries that would come to prove absolutely decisive. One of these was the tool I've named the stress map, which I used to eliminate my chronic stress (see page 123) and the other was meditation. My problem was that my brain would never shut up. Thoughts were always buzzing around in there, left and right, all over the place – I couldn't get any peace! Now this is a problem in itself, but what made it even worse for me was that most of those thoughts were negative, critical or destructive. I was drinking hundreds, if not thousands, of Devil's cocktails every day. Each thought was boosting my stress levels, and I couldn't make them stop. That is, until the day when I learned how to meditate. Earlier on, I explained how meditation can be seen as a way to insert a delay in your responses to stimuli. Before I started to meditate, I felt the full force of every negative thought that entered my mind, but after just four weeks of meditation practice, I was able to acknowledge my thoughts, insert that delay between stimulus and response, and use the time in between to decide how to feel about the thought.

Let's give this a go together! I'll describe how I usually perform a focus meditation, and you can give it a try for five minutes. If you're already an experienced meditator, you'll probably know all about this stuff, but you could still give it those five minutes just for the enjoyment of doing it.

1. Sit up, ideally in a lotus position, with your back against a wall or on a chair. If you sit too comfortably or lie down, you'll risk falling asleep instead of meditating.

2. Relax your whole body, your legs, your arms and, particularly, your jaw and your tongue.

3. Keep your eyes still. It's more difficult to think with your eyes held still, and we want to be doing less thinking for this meditation.

4. Take three deep breaths, and follow each with a long exhalation.

5. Close your eyes, and continue to take deep breaths, inhaling and exhaling slowly (go for seven breaths per minute).

6. Say the word 'out' silently to yourself on your exhalation, and say the word 'in' silently to yourself on your inhalation.

7. When a thought comes to you – and it will – the moment you become aware of it, you should simply visualize sending it away in your mind. Send it to the right, or to the left, up or down – it doesn't matter.

8. An incredibly important detail here is that you're not to judge yourself or feel bad for having thoughts entering your mind every second. My record for going without any thoughts is thirty seconds, and that's after years of practising meditation. At first, they came every second, often two at a time.

Once you find your rhythm in meditation, it can feel absolutely wondrous. Your Angel's cocktail will fill up with mood-boosting serotonin and energizing dopamine, and be topped up with a dose of GABA, Gamma-aminobutyric acid, which slows the brain down and can make us feel a little high. You'll also experience a pleasant lowering of your cortisol levels, which will help you feel more relaxed. It's very rare for anybody to find their rhythm the first time they meditate, but if you keep practising every day, you'll get there before you know it! I meditated for twenty minutes each day for the first six months. Although the short-term sensations while you're actually meditating can be glorious, the truly amazing effects are the long-term ones. Meditation prevents anxiety and stress, provides pain relief, helps you limit your negative thinking, alleviates symptoms of depression, makes you feel less lonely, boosts your social engagement, aids self-awareness, enhances your creativity, improves your focus, aids your memory and makes you more compassionate. It's available to you any-time, anywhere – and it's absolutely free! The best part is that you don't even have to spend much time doing it. Stud-ies have shown that powerful effects can be achieved by meditating for just thirteen minutes a day for eight weeks. All you need to do is start establishing the habit! If you feel that you don't have the time, that's just a sign that you're in especial need of meditation.

Focus meditation, gratitude meditation and observation meditation are the three most common kinds of meditation, and they all follow the same basic process I outlined above. The difference is what you do during the actual meditation.

During focus meditation, you focus on your breathing or heartbeat until you feel ready to let go and allow your mind to roam free.

During gratitude meditation, you focus on feeling gratitude for everything, everybody and yourself. Allow your mind to drift from one person in your life to the next and say thank you. Allow your mind to drift from one experience to the next and say thank you. Allow your mind to drift from one part of your body to the next and say thank you. Gratitude meditation has been shown to have the specific benefit of making us more compassionate to others. So if that's an area where you feel you have particular room for improvement, this is the right form of meditation for you.

Observation meditation emphasizes distancing yourself from whatever thought you're thinking, and considering it from afar. You have the thoughts, but you practise not judging them, and then sending them away again. This particular form of meditation is great when you want to increase the time before responding to stimuli and would like to dial down your own powerful emotional responses. More self-control, less judgement and less evaluation – those are the most common effects achieved by observation meditation.

Spontaneous Meditation

Meditation can also be done as opportune moments arise during your day. For me this tends to happen when I go diving, when I shower and sometimes when I take a walk. Consider when you tend to meditate spontaneously, and see if you could fit more of it in. Ideally you should complement this practice with daily focus meditations.

Creative Meditation

If you have children or are young, you're bound to remember the fidget-spinner fad. These are small toys that you can spin with your fingers, which can keep going for up to a couple of minutes. One day, I brought home a particularly flashy spinner, which could keep spinning for a full three minutes. I told Leona, my daughter, about something that I called fidget meditation. Being an avid fan of all things fidget spinner, she was rather keen to give it a try. I told her to lie down on the floor, placed the fidget spinner on her forehead and set it spinning. Her job was to lie still with her eyes shut, and feel the fidget spinner move until it stopped. Three minutes later, she opened her eyes with a slightly dazed look on her face, and said, 'That was great! Can I do it again?' That was Leona's introduction to meditation, and she even got her friends to try it.

In the next section, I'll help you make better sense of your Angel's cocktail by giving a summary of all the things we've gone over so far, and telling you how you can easily mix a cocktail for yourself every morning and evening, or at any other time you feel like it. There are no side effects — just more wonder to add to your life.

Angel's and Devil's Cocktails

The bartender leans over the counter, and asks what you're having.

'I'd like an Angel's cocktail of testosterone and endorphins, thanks.'

'Wow! Is it a special occasion?'

'Yes, it is! This is the first day of the rest of my life, so I'd love a boost of confidence from the testosterone and euphoria from the endorphins. That feels like the right mix for me!'

'Sounds good! Go for it!'

To make this easier for you, and to save you a lot of flipping back and forth between different pages, I've summarized, in the following chart, the six substances we've discussed so far, and how you can produce them using the tools I've given you. If you'd like a digital, colourful version that you can print and put on your wall at home, scan the QR code on page 186. It will take you to davidjpphillips.com, and the resource package page for this book, where you'll be able to download it free of charge.

Dopamine	Oxytocin	Serotonin	Endorphins	Testosterone	Cortisol (to reduce)
Emotional whys	Hugs	Satisfaction	Smiling	Wins	Relaxation
Momentum	Touch	Daylight	Laughing	Belief in a win	Meditation
Vision board	Eye contact	Diet	Spicy food	Music	Reducing anxiety
Cold-water bathing	Good sex	Mindfulness	Exercise	The body	The stress map
Dopamine balancing	Heat	Reducing inflammation	Music	Muscle building	Oxytocin
Dopamine stacking	Cold	Meditation	Chocolate	Aggression	Reducing inflammation
Portioned dopamine	Generosity	Sex	Dancing	Sports	Exercise
Internal vs external	Soothing music	Social status	Movies	Movies	Breathing

Dopamine variability	Empathy	Smiling	Pictures	Pictures	Changing your perspective
Expectations	Gratitude	Laughing	Sex	Sex	Dopamine vs cortisol
Socialization	*Ho'oponopono*	Exercise	Memories	Exercise	Breaking the pattern
Books	Books	Memories		Memories	False truths
Movies	Movies				Conflicting truths
Pictures	Pictures				Sex
Sex	Meditation				Memories
Exercise	Memories				
Meditation					
Memories					

Scan the code to download a colourful version of this chart. You'll also find the resource package for this book, which includes inspiring videos, illustrations and sample guided meditations!

So What Next?

There are several amazing paths you could choose for making future Angel's cocktails, and what follows is a list of some of my best tips for you.

Establish a Morning Routine

A good start to the day is key to becoming your best version of yourself. Choose one tool for each substance and design your own morning ritual. Make a step-by-step plan and carry it out every morning you're able to.

1. Look at your vision board and experience a motivating emotion based on it (read more about this in the chapter on dopamine on page 46).

2. Do something kind for somebody you care about – call them, send them a text message or record a video and send it to them (oxytocin).
3. Go out into the sun as soon as possible in the morning, and think back on positive memories (positive cortisol + serotonin).
4. Exercise, or listen to a good podcast or show (serotonin + endorphins + dopamine).
5. Decide that today is going to be a day of wins for you (testosterone).
6. Meditate or do some breathing exercises (stress relief).

The Stress Map

If you haven't already done it, fill in your stress map in accordance with the instructions on page 124, and then eliminate or resolve as many of the entries as you can. You could ask a friend to help by giving you their view on the entries, as this can help you find new solutions. Fill in a new stress map every six months, as some stressors sneak up on us without making themselves known at first (refer to the example on page 125).

Priming

'Priming' means preparing something for activation. Here, it means that you'll be preparing a tailored meditation for yourself, in which you will address each of the six substances. Like most meditations, this begins with relaxing your body, breathing slow, deep breaths and relaxing your face. After this, once you've attained a state of calm, you can embark on your mental meditation, in which you address each substance in turn. Here's an example of how this might go:

1. Recall past experiences you've had of gratitude, love and caring (oxytocin).
2. Recall past experiences you've had of happiness, harmony, calm and satisfaction (serotonin).
3. Recall past experiences you've had of pride and self-love (serotonin).
4. Recall past experiences you've had of laughter and smiles (endorphins).
5. Recall past experiences you've had of motivation, and think of future motivation and future successes you could experience (dopamine).
6. Recall past experiences you've had of power, struggles, wins, success and confidence (testosterone).

The order matters here, because the initial deep breathing and relaxation will reduce your stress levels, and the meditation that follows is structured to help you gradually intensify your emotional reactions, building towards a powerful climax. You can amplify this meditation by matching it to music. If you're as ambitious as a friend of mine, you could edit your own soundtrack, in which each substance gets its own two-minute section of a song that you've hand-picked to match the specific memories you'll be thinking of.

Choose a Favourite

A simple way to start your day is to practise triggering a specific substance that you want to experience more of, and then carrying out relevant exercises several times throughout the day. It's OK to choose two, but you should avoid going for three or more, as this can easily get too confusing. Here are some guiding principles that can help you choose which substance to practise triggering. Once you've made your choice, you can always return to the chapter in question and study the tools I've listed again. When you feel ready, just go for it!

- If you feel lacking in pride and self-love – serotonin
- If you feel lacking in motivation and drive – dopamine
- If you feel lacking in confidence in some particular domain or area – testosterone
- If you feel lacking in energy and focus – dopamine
- If you feel lacking in happiness – the stress map (cortisol) + serotonin
- If you feel lacking in sexual drive – the tools for stress relief (cortisol)
- If you feel lacking in presence – oxytocin and serotonin

Give to Others

There are a couple of interesting things involved in giving somebody else an Angel's cocktail. The first of these is that many of us tend to be more prepared to give to others when we feel more content with ourselves and our own lives. The second aspect is that when we give to others, it gives us an opportunity to experience their reactions and share in their emotions. It's a genuine win-win situation!

Do you have children? Are you a leader? Do you have friends? If so, that means that you have lots of people you can practise on. Look at the chart of Angel's cocktail techniques and choose one to give to somebody else. You could offer them a compliment, a helping hand or a deliberate boost to their social status by acknowledging them in the presence of others. Being generous and helping others can feel magical, and it will release large amounts of oxytocin for your own Angel's cocktail.

Categorize Your Friends

People often laugh at this example at first, but usually it slowly dawns on them that it's actually pretty ingenious. The idea here is to categorize your friends by substance. Once you've done this, you'll have a better understanding of whom to talk to when you need a refill of a specific substance. I've had this substance talk with most of my close friends, and I've also had conversations with them about the substances they feel that they trigger by talking to me.

I call Marcus because he adds levity to my life. I'm almost always brimming with endorphins and serotonin when we've finished talking. The endorphins come from the way we laugh at everything together. He provides me with serotonin by being great at lifting my spirits and giving me some healthy perspective on my perceived social status.

I call Maria when I need to remind myself of what it truly means to be human, and what it feels like to genuinely care about other people. She produces more oxytocin in me than anybody else.

I call Krister, my friend the forester, when I feel the need for some grounding. Sometimes my dopamine-starved brain drifts away and flies off too high above the clouds, but fifteen minutes of speaking to Krister, who cuts down trees and moves logs around in the woods with his forwarder, always brings me back down to terra firma. Life is quite simple really, if you ask Krister.

I call Magnus when I need to slow things down. He's incredibly focused on serotonin, and takes his time even when things get hectic. He's better at enjoying a cup of coffee than anybody else I know. We're probably each other's absolute opposites, and whenever I meet him it helps me realize that my dopamine isn't just making me fly too high – it's making me run too fast too.

Focus Questions

The things we focus on produce emotions in us, and the quality of these emotions influences the quality of our decisions. The quality of our decisions, in turn, influences our quality of life. For this reason, it's important to keep track of what you're focusing on. We humans make sense of the world around us by formulating statements and questions. For example, we might think to ourselves, *Oh, so-and-so must be terribly busy*, or *Wow, so-and-so's car is dirty!*, or *What's wrong with this?*, or *What's wrong with me?* Internal questions tend to have a stronger emotional impact on us than statements, because the questions dig a little deeper. This is why we should address them first. Besides, successfully altering our recurring internal questions tends to bring with it the effect of also changing our internal statements.

I refer to these questions as focus questions. If your focus questions are positive, they will add positive ingredients to your Angel's cocktail. For example, the focus question 'how can I be more present?' could increase your oxytocin, while 'what's good about me?' could potentially increase your serotonin. At the same time, negative focus questions such as 'what's wrong with this?' or 'what is the world coming to?' are more likely to feed you a Devil's cocktail. As the main priority of our brains is to keep us alive, it's far more common for people to have negative focus questions than to have positive ones. As a consequence, we can quite quickly achieve positive effects by reformulating our focus questions in more positive ways. In the countless self-leadership courses I have given with my team, we've collected more than a thousand different focus questions from our participants. Below are the eight most common, and I've suggested how they can be turned into positive focus questions instead.

What's wrong with this?	What's good about this?
What would have happened if I didn't . . . ?	How can I learn from this?
What's wrong with me?	What's good about me?
What's going to happen next?	How can I be more present right now?
Is it OK for me to be different?	How can I inspire others?
How could this harm me?	How can I challenge myself?
How can I make things even better for me?	How can I enjoy what I already have?
Am I good enough for my partner?	How can I be my best self?

Perhaps you can find your own focus question among these examples. If not, identify it on your own, and then use it to understand how to begin listening to yourself. As soon as you discover that you have a recurring internal question that is negative, you should sit down and figure out which positive question you could replace it with. Next, you start the process of repetition. Repeat the positive question to yourself often for an extended period of time and your focus question will eventually change, along with your internal cocktail. I used to be unable to enter a room or meet a new person without triggering my own negative focus question: 'what's wrong with this?' This single focus question played a major role in what would later lead to my struggle with depression. Asking yourself 'what's wrong with this?' hundreds of times each day is unlikely to produce any positive emotions, and it definitely won't produce an Angel's cocktail. Eventually I managed to replace that question with 'what's fantastic about this?' The effect of this change, after I cemented it by repeating it stubbornly for a few months, was astounding.

Angel's Cocktail – Bar Open 24 Hours

Welcome to the Angel's cocktail bar! What can I get you? As you've probably understood by now, there is more than one kind of Angel's cocktail. It's time for you to strap on your bartender braces, twirl your moustache and mix up twelve different useful cocktails.

Before a Job Interview or Date
(Testosterone, Oxytocin)

Boost your testosterone and confidence by recalling past successes and wins. Ideally combine this with music that makes you feel successful, invincible and bold. Walk, stand and move as though you own the world. Feel free to add a dose of oxytocin to optimize the effect. For example, you could watch a video clip that triggers your empathy and moves you.

Effective Studying (Dopamine, Testosterone)

When you study, you need to maintain a strong focus and give yourself the best possible conditions for remembering what you've studied. Dopamine can help you with this. For example, you could trigger it by thinking of the positive outcomes that studying will bring you, or how much fun it will be for you to learn more about the subject in question. If this doesn't work, you can also boost your dopamine by exercising before studying. It's also important to reduce your access to fast dopamine and cortisol by leaving your smartphone or tablet in another room. Dopamine will serve you best over short sessions, so you should spend forty to sixty minutes studying, and then take a break to recharge. To boost your confidence when studying, you can also stimulate testosterone releases by celebrating your wins as you go, maybe after each passed exam.

Before Social Events
(Endorphins, Testosterone, Oxytocin)

When you're about to attend social events of any kind, you can benefit from boosting these three prosocial substances. Start by watching something that triggers laughter and endorphins for half an hour, like funny video clips on your smartphone. On the way to your social event, you can boost your testosterone by listening to encouraging, uplifting music. Once you arrive, you can release oxytocin by striking up a conversation with somebody who genuinely interests you. Avoid people who you know will negatively impact your perceived social status and serotonin, i.e. people who make you feel inferior in some way.

Manage Conflicts (Oxytocin, Serotonin, Dopamine)

When we sense a conflict brewing, this increases our stress levels, which impacts our ability to think clearly. To prevent this, you could try activating your parasympathetic nervous system and directly and indirectly upping your oxytocin levels by relaxing your body and breathing calmly, patting or stroking yourself in a reassuring way or just holding a cup with a hot drink in it. A common instinct in conflicts is to 'return the favour' by reducing the other person's serotonin levels to ensure that they will suffer pain too. We do this by belittling them, deflating their social status or bringing up irrelevant flaws they possess or mistakes they've made. It's a good idea to avoid such behaviour, as it only distances you further from each other and makes the other person defensive. We ought to approach conflict as an opportunity for growth, inner development and learning more about the people we spend our lives with. To help you do this, it can be a good idea to prepare with a dose of dopamine: explore your emotional whys in relation to the conflict, think about how good it will feel when it is resolved and consider how the conflict itself might represent a positive opportunity to improve your relationship with the other person.

Increase Your Creativity (Dopamine, Serotonin)

When we want to do creative work, the good mood we get from serotonin and the drive we get from dopamine make a fantastic combination. The easiest way to access these substances is by taking some exercise or a cold-water bath or both. The creative process tends to occur in two stages. The first of these involves gathering ideas. The best approach for this is to visit new places, meet new people and take in new knowledge. All three of these activities stimulate and are stimulated by dopamine. The second stage involves sitting down to fit your new ideas and impressions together into whatever it is you're creating. Another interesting way that dopamine can factor in here is by creating momentum. If you're having a hard time getting started, even after exercising, taking a cold-water bath and taking in new impressions, the best idea can often be to just jump right in anyway. You see, dopamine tends to lead to even more dopamine. As soon as your creativity gets going, even just a little, your dopamine flow will begin to feed itself.

Fall Asleep Quicker (Oxytocin, Cortisol)

It's basically impossible to fall asleep with excessive stress levels raging through your body. When your thoughts are racing, your brain is being bombarded with images and sensory impressions, and you find yourself tossing and turning, you're simply not going to manage to go to sleep. The most effective way of exiting this state is to boost your oxytocin levels and activate your parasympathetic nervous system. This is best achieved by getting ten minutes of meditation in before bedtime. Another option here is to take a warm shower or bath. After this, lie down in bed and breathe calmly. Aim for six to eight breaths a minute or fewer, and try to feel your body begin to relax. Keep your eyes still behind your eyelids if you can. I promise that this will make a difference. You should also try to avoid cortisol-inducing activities before bedtime, like working at your computer or watching and reading materials that produce stress in you. There are plenty of other useful tips for sleep, but these are the most important.

Wake Up Fresh and Rested (Dopamine, Oxytocin)

When you wake up, your cortisol levels will be naturally high to give you the energy you need to get going. But you can expose yourself to sunlight to amplify this effect by taking a twenty-minute walk first thing in the morning. Feel free to combine this with dopamine by thinking ahead to something fun or entertaining that you have planned for the day. If you can't think of anything that fits the bill, you should come up with some exciting plan or other that you can look forward to. It could be something as simple as buying your first ice cream of the year, visiting a coffee place you haven't tried before, practising something or other or calling a friend. When you get home, combine this dopamine with a nice dose of oxytocin that you can trigger by lying down for a minute and feeling grateful about something that happened yesterday – it could be something somebody said or did, or some experience you had.

Celebrate Better and More Often
(Testosterone, Serotonin)

Far too many of us forget to celebrate things or don't celebrate enough. The advantage of having the 'right' amount of celebrations is that it will encourage you to celebrate more often. My first piece of advice here is for you to celebrate more often, even your small successes, like finishing a walk, daring to venture outside your comfort zone, managing to be mindful or getting somebody to smile. My second piece of advice is to make an effort to feel genuine pride in your achievements. You can trigger this sense of pride by standing up tall, relishing the moment and focusing on the positive feelings you have about what you just did. By celebrating achievements large and small, you can boost your confidence by triggering testosterone, and by celebrating the way you feel, you can boost your self-esteem and serotonin levels.

Falling in Love (Oxytocin, Serotonin,
Dopamine, Cortisol, Endorphins)

However odd this may sound, it's possible to prepare the ground for love to spark. You can begin by triggering oxytocin by engaging in prolonged eye contact with somebody. Ask personal questions and listen actively, while sharing your own personal experiences with them. Touch them, briefly at first. Once you're confident they will allow it, you can move on to slightly longer touches. Giving compliments can help – this elevates their perceived social status, which is likely to have a positive impact on their serotonin levels. If you can get them to laugh, this will release endorphins and make them feel more relaxed and prosocial. You could also consider artificially raising their stress levels to produce a state that their body can interpret as arousal. Good ways of doing this include watching horror films together or riding roller coasters – that kind of thing. That way they will be more likely to associate the way they feel with you. This is one of the processes that's often involved when people fall in love.

Making Better Decisions (Dopamine, Cortisol)

When are we best prepared to make difficult decisions? It's a tricky question. If you make decisions that might impact your future when you're high on dopamine and feeling like you could take on the world, you could well end up feeling rather anxious later on when you consider the unrealistic commitments you've made to yourself and others. On the other hand, if you make decisions when your dopamine levels are low, you might be too pessimistic and cautious to seize the opportunities that could actually improve your life. I recommend making important decisions at times when your dopamine levels are close to their average. This will mean that your decisions reflect your average emotional state and should improve the probability that you'll be able to deliver on your decisions without suffering adverse effects. Another suggestion would be to avoid making decisions when you're in a state of stress, as decisions made in this state will tend to revolve around immediate relief from pain

rather than any considerations of long-term consequences. To conclude: ideally you should make important
decisions when your serotonin and cortisol levels are
close to normal.

Doing Something Difficult (Serotonin, Dopamine, Testosterone, Oxytocin, Endorphins)

Doing something difficult, like giving a presentation if
you're shy, or giving feedback if you're conflict-averse, can
often feel challenging, as it requires a lot of willpower and
energy. Here are my best tips for handling this. Utilize your
naturally high serotonin levels in the morning, and get
your difficult task out of the way before lunchtime. Apart
from providing you with relief, this will send you on to the
rest of your day feeling great about yourself. You can also
produce dopamine in advance by thinking about your
expected positive outcome rather than producing cortisol
by focusing on how difficult you imagine it will be. You
might also benefit from raising your testosterone levels, as
this will reduce your impulse control and boost your confidence. A good way of doing this can be to listen to music
that you find encouraging and emboldening. After this,
move on to mentally visualizing what it will be like when
you've achieved your desired outcome, and if it seems
reasonable, trigger some testosterone by invoking your
aggression as a response to what's getting in the way of
your ambitions. If the difficult thing you're about to do
causes you stress, amp up your oxytocin levels – you can
try doing this by relaxing and taking deep, calm breaths.

Finally, if it feels right to you, you can add some endorphins to the process too for their pain-relieving effect by laughing and smiling.

A good example of a challenging activity is the cold-water bath I coach people through. Because I know it can be difficult, I schedule it for first thing in the morning (serotonin) and encourage them to focus on how proud they will feel about their achievement after taking the cold-water bath rather than on how painful they expect it to be (dopamine). Just before they get in the water, I ask them to produce feelings of boldness and strength, and stand up tall (testosterone). When they're in the water, I ask them to breathe calmly (oxytocin), and while they focus on remaining there, I ask them to laugh and smile (endorphins), which helps them relax. Afterwards, I make a point of encouraging them to celebrate having passed the challenge (serotonin, testosterone).

Motivation (Dopamine, Testosterone)

We can either produce genuine motivation or fake it. Let's start by taking a look at genuine motivation. This is easiest to produce by thinking about what you're trying to achieve and by enjoying the activity itself. If you need to rake leaves, but don't feel like doing it, you can imagine how great your lawn is going to look and how good you'll feel about yourself when you're done. You should also take the opportunity to enjoy the experience itself. Pay attention to any emotions you might experience as you see your lawn improve as a result of your raking efforts. Avoid dopamine stacking by listening to a podcast while you work – this would essentially constitute relying on fake motivation for no good reason. Dopamine is particularly powerful when combined with testosterone. It can be a good idea to boost it ahead of time by focusing on the win, listening to emboldening and empowering music, and walking, standing and moving as though the world belonged to you. It's also important to treat every step along the way to a raked lawn as a victory, and to celebrate them all!

Now let's see how you can utilize fake motivation. The interesting thing about emotions is that your brain isn't particularly good at telling where specific emotions come from. This means that you can construct your motivation from one point of view, and then use it for a completely different purpose. For example, you could do some exercise before you do something you don't fancy doing, like raking leaves. The undesirable activity will be far easier for you to engage in after some exercise, as your dopamine levels will be elevated. You should do your best to avoid the opposite strategy: lazing around for two hours before heading out to do the raking. The contrast between fast and slow dopamine can be quite overwhelming, even for the most disciplined among us, and this approach would make you very likely to come to a quick change of mind and head back to the couch and your social media feed almost immediately.

Devil's Cocktail

'I'd like a Devil's cocktail, please!' Are there really people out there who would order one of those? Strangely enough, there are. However, in the majority of cases, people drink Devil's cocktails without even realizing that this is what they're doing. Let's take a look at the six most common variants of a Devil's cocktail.

Variant 1: Unintentional

Variant one is the unintentional Devil's cocktail. This person could be suffering from chronic inflammation or have been experiencing intense emotional or physical struggles for quite some time. Even if they never realize this, the effects of the stress caused by the inflammation or pain will tend to make their mood deteriorate gradually as time goes by.

Variant 2: Innocent

Variant two is a more innocent case. This is somebody who doesn't permit themselves to feel or express positive emotions. Rather, their lives remain more or less consistently melancholy affairs. Often they were simply never taught how to express, experience or communicate positive emotions. In other instances, the cause could be trauma they suffered earlier in their lives. However, as is always the case in self-leadership, it's still possible to learn to find the courage to feel, show and express emotions.

Variant 3: Passive

These people are more or less deliberate in their choices but struggle with passivity. These are people who live for the weekend and approach their work weeks as nothing but drudgery that they have to get through. During the week they remain more or less emotionally shut down, because they either don't enjoy what they do or fail to see the point of it. Although their situation could also be caused by bullies in their workplace or school. The emotional shutdown and lack of Angel's cocktail ingredients they experience during the weeks make their weekends seem like their only oases in life. Unfortunately, Monday inevitably comes rolling round again, and their lives go right back to being miserable. This variant is, essentially, down to a shortage of Angel's cocktail ingredients in their lives.

Variant 4: Active

This Devil's cocktail is a very common one. The basic ingredient here is chronic stress caused by an unsustainable situation in someone's professional or personal life. Constant stress for months or years on end can affect an individual's natural balance of dopamine (drive and pleasure), serotonin (satisfaction and self-esteem), testosterone, progesterone and oestrogen (sex hormones), which will, in turn, affect areas such as their sex drive and confidence.

Variant 5: Dark

The saddest kind of Devil's cocktail is when somebody behaves like Voldemort from the Harry Potter books and utilizes the 'dark' powers that each substance can provide. For example, these people produce connectedness by putting down other groups (dark oxytocin); they use various techniques for dominance to improve their own social status (dark serotonin); and they rob others of testosterone by claiming their wins and successes for themselves.

Variant 6: Lost

This fairly common type is a person who casts themselves in the role of 'victim'. These people are lost and have hooked themselves up to a self-destructive source of serotonin (social status) and oxytocin (connectedness). They deliberately put themselves down and create problems for themselves, and then bask in the attention that their sorry states bring them. They don't just get attention either – their fellow humans and friends will often show them compassion and try to help them. This becomes a way for them to feel acknowledged and experience closeness (oxytocin). Unfortunately this is a trap that can be quite easy to end up in but which is often far from easy to escape without outside assistance.

Devil's Cocktail – A Summary

Most people have a mix of Devil's and Angel's cocktails in their lives. They lead lives that are OK and acceptable in general, but they still carry around some unfulfilled wish or a sense that they could be getting more from life.

For somebody who drinks far more Devil's cocktails than Angel's cocktails, life can seem to be shrouded in fog, but getting to that point happens so gradually that they barely notice it. As time goes by, and they accept their daily Devil's cocktails, these individuals will begin to feel increasingly drained and hollow. This can often lead to recurring self-criticism, which will only further amplify their negative emotions. Eventually this can make them compensate for these emotions by feeding themselves fast dopamine of various kinds, by excessively indulging in smartphone use, gaming, sweets, snacks, unhealthy takeaway food, news, pornography or social media. This is often accompanied by reduced social stimulation and a reduction in physical activity. If things get really bad, these people can start feeling so hopeless that their need for dopamine-based stimulation drives them to develop addictions to gambling, food, alcohol or other activities. Long-term overconsumption of Devil's cocktails can cause a person to become dysphoric and develop symptoms of depression or anxiety. It's also likely that they won't have a clue about what to do to change their situation.

This might sound like bad news if you're one of those people who's been downing too many Devil's cocktails for too long. But I also have good news for you. Whichever of the variants above you happen to identify with, you can always choose to start downing Angel's cocktails instead! Regardless of your situation, this will make a difference, and as time goes by, you'll find that it keeps getting easier. The fog will eventually lift, and the bubble you felt trapped inside will burst when you feel life return to you.

My best pieces of advice for breaking free of the habitual overconsumption of daily Devil's cocktails are:

1. Use the stress map, and take immediate action based on what it reveals to you. You can read more about it in the chapter on cortisol on page 123.
2. Reduce your fast dopamine intake, and replace it with slow dopamine by using the tools in the chapter on dopamine, see page 32.
3. Implement the tools in the chapter on oxytocin beginning on page 56.

4. Practise self-love and reduce self-critical tendencies by using the tools in the chapter on serotonin on page 91.

Alongside these four steps, you should introduce regular exercise to your life, even if it's only short walks. Meditate daily and optimize your sleep using the tools on page 171.

PART TWO
Making Your Own Future

Welcome to the second part of the book! Now, don't let the fact that this part is quite short and simple deceive you. Leonardo da Vinci supposedly said that simplicity is the ultimate sophistication, and that's the mindset you should bring to this second part. It is short and it is simple, but its contents are absolutely essential for learning to make Angel's cocktails that will last for the rest of your life.

There are two different attitudes you can take to music. On the one hand, you can make music, which is active, and, on the other hand, you can listen to music, which is passive. So far we've been learning how to make music. For example, we've gone through how to mix up our own Angel's cocktails by laughing to release endorphins, giving ourselves little wins to release testosterone, and hugging each other to release oxytocin. Now it's time to learn how to listen to music, i.e. train our brains to produce endorphins, testosterone and oxytocin passively without any deliberate effort on our part.

I'd like you to join me on a cool evening one July, just as the sun is beginning to set on the horizon. The sunset is bathing the wheat field in front of you in a warm amber glow. You can feel a light summer breeze coming in across the wheat field, and you decide to wander to the other side through the lush vegetation. A short while later, you've arrived and turn back to look the way you came, but you can barely see a trace of your passing. It was such a pleasant walk that you decide to take it again and again, and by the end of the summer you've probably taken it at least 100 times, forging a clearer path each time you cross. Now imagine that for some reason you walked across the wheat field 100,000 times. What kind of path would that leave behind? It would be one that was easy to follow, which took very little energy to walk, and which you wouldn't mind taking, as you'd feel very accustomed to it and very secure in choosing it. That's a very precise analogy for how your habitual thoughts and behaviours are actually formed. Each recurring thought, truth or behaviour is a path, and you've trodden along some of them tens – or even hundreds – of thousands of times. You're accustomed to your thoughts and behaviours. They represent safe, simple and energy-efficient routes for you to take.

But suppose that one day you thought to yourself: *I'm tired of always taking this path across the wheat field; it's not getting me to where I want to go. I'm going to forge a new path!* So you walk fifty paces to the left, and start treading a new path instead. It's awkward and hard going. The wheat keeps snapping back at you, and you stumble over lumps of earth and rocks. Your brain complains to you: *Come on! What is this foolishness? Why are we walking this way, when there's a safe, well-trodden path just over there?* But you've made up your mind, and eventually the change comes. Because what happens to a path that's no longer used? It becomes overgrown. After a while the new path will become the quicker, simpler option. And after you've walked along

214

your new path a sufficient number of times, there will be barely any sign that the old one ever existed. Sometimes reading old journal entries can remind us of old behaviours that once preoccupied us and felt like major challenges to overcome, but which have now been completely erased from our lives.

I hope this metaphor will help you understand that all your thoughts, truths and behaviours can potentially be replaced by new ones, as long as you repeat the new ones enough times. The same, of course, is true of newer behaviours. Take, say, a habit like smiling more often. Genuine smiles can feed you a magical combination of dopamine, serotonin and endorphins. If you decide to practise smiling more frequently, you'll be treading up new paths inside your brain whenever you do so, and one day, a few months or perhaps a year later, you'll suddenly notice that you're smiling more often, without even giving it any thought. Congratulations! You've learned to listen to music instead of having to actively create it. You're mixing up passive Angel's cocktails for yourself without even having to think about triggering anything. The scientific term for this concept is *neuroplasticity*.

Neuroplasticity and Repetition

For a very long time the consensus was that the human brain was static and unchangeable, and there are still people who insist that they were somehow born without the ability to dance, cook, find their way around, be funny, be good presenters, lead others, close a sale and so on. This attitude radically inhibits – sometimes completely – an individual's growth in the related areas. According to Carol Dweck's work, this is referred to as having a *fixed mindset*. On the other hand, anybody who believes that they can improve and grow in a certain area actually *can* do just that. This is called having a *growth mindset*. We've learned not only that the brain is malleable, but that we can also decide for ourselves when and if we want it to change.

Ask yourself if you think you're free to choose happiness, pride, self-love and confidence. If you believe that you are, then you are! If, however, you believe that you don't enjoy that freedom, you should find a way to convince yourself otherwise. You may be on a longer path, but there's nothing impossible about it. Read on with an open mind, and discuss the matter with friends who are curious and open-minded, and seem to have a growth mindset. Take inspiration from them and change your outlook. Humans are so open to influence that we can be led to believe almost anything. In this case, it's a question of believing that you have the power to change your behaviour and influence your own well-being.

Suppose you were to contract some mysterious tropical disease that made it necessary for you to be quarantined in a specialist hospital for twelve weeks. You are led into a bare white room with a small window facing a brick wall. You receive your meals through a hatch at the far side of the room. The staff are good enough to provide you with a computer, to provide you with some entertainment. It's lonely, I suppose, but it's not an intolerable situation. One day, when you're reading the news, you come across a scientific study that has apparently shown that red-headed individuals have become prone to extreme fits of violence because of changes to their genetic make-up caused by recent atmospheric changes. The article cautions you against making eye contact with red-headed people. After this, over the next twelve weeks, you go on to read a long list of news stories about violent crimes apparently committed by red-headed people. Finally the day arrives when it's deemed safe for you to rejoin the general population, and you are released from the ward. At the entrance to the hospital, you walk by a red-headed man and find yourself flinching. This might seem like a strange example – who on earth would choose to publish those kinds of lies and manipulate the news to make red-headed people look bad? But if you give it some thought, you'll soon realize that this is how the news media and social media actually work. They make you believe things you would never have believed otherwise, and which you're not even really aware of believing. The media, for example, tends to emphasize negative news over positive news, which can give us a skewed idea about the true state of the world. What happened during these twelve weeks is that you underwent a neurological change, which caused your brain to automatically serve you up a Devil's cocktail at the mere sight of a red-headed person.

My point is that whatever you feed your brain with, it will end up becoming your 'truth' if you keep consuming it for long enough. If you haven't taken charge of what you'll allow your brain to be fed with before now, that means your beliefs have been chosen for you by your parents, your friends, your culture, the conventional media you've consumed and social media. Your brain is being constantly fed with ideas (programmed), both consciously and subconsciously, by the people you choose to associate with. The things you choose to input into your brain on a daily basis form paths through your mental wheat field, which, in turn, determine which cocktail you end up with. Neuroplasticity never rests. It is this process that continuously adapts your brain to ensure you'll function optimally in any circumstances you happen to find yourself in. This ongoing process has shaped you into the individual you are. In technical terms, the memories and activities (nerve connections and neurons) that you repeat frequently will be reinforced, while the ones you don't repeat frequently will be weakened. This means that physical changes occur in your brain as a result of your choice of whether to repeat something or not. In other words, you can create permanent, automatic Angel's cocktails within yourself by making the right choices about what to feed your brain with.

How Long Does Change Take?

In all likelihood, the change is already under way within you. The tips and ideas you've read in this book may have already inspired you to tread new paths through your wheat field. Change can come as an epiphany, when something suddenly falls into place or makes sense. But insights like that can also be fleeting, and they're difficult to produce and predict on demand. A better idea, then, is to rely on the predictable but slower mechanics of repetition. Studies into neuroplasticity have found that visible differences exist in the brain after just four weeks, and that these differences only become greater and greater as time goes by. Most studies of this particular phenomenon haven't gone on for more than twelve weeks, but the few longer ones that have been conducted show quite clearly that the changes carry on after that point. However, based on this science and on my own experiences, there seems to me to be a magical time frame of about eight weeks. After this time, the exercises begin to be activated passively, i.e. without any need for deliberate triggering on your part. In other words, after eight weeks of effort you'll be able to begin listening to the music you've created. It took between four and forty weeks for the various tools I use to become automated. Nobody can really say for sure how long it will take for you to bring about lasting change in some behaviour or habitual thinking pattern. It varies a lot from person to person, and depends on a variety of factors, including genetics, epigenetics (how your behaviours and environment can cause changes that affect the way your genes work), existing programming, whether a *growth* mindset or a *fixed* mindset is present, how often the exercises are repeated, how long they are repeated for and the specifics of each individual's living situation. What we do know, though, without any doubt, is that you will definitely be able to reprogramme yourself. It makes no difference whether it takes you two, eight or twelve months. How long it takes isn't the point. What matters is that you decide that from now on you'll be making the active choice to put in the training to feel and be the way you want to. I've been free from my depressive thoughts for almost six years now, and the most exciting part of my journey so far is the fact that every morning, upon waking, I have looked at my vision board, which is right by my bed, chosen a tool to work on for the day and continued repeating this pattern over and over. I've kept feeling better with each year that has gone by. Sometimes I wonder if things will ever stop getting better. Sure, I have my bad days, just like anyone, but now – knowing how to break the pattern of them – I am more often than not genuinely high on life!

A New Life

You, I and everybody else have to face the fact that the world we live in is complicated for us. The news stories we are fed every day, the extreme social constructs we compare ourselves to, the infinity of options we're presented with, the lack of natural exercise in our lifestyles, the focus on performance, the temptations of fast food and sugar that only cause us to crave more carbohydrates and sugar, helicopter-parented kids who demand more stimulation than any generation before them – all these phenomena present mental challenges. It could even be that our world is more difficult to live in than the one Duncan and Grace inhabited 25,000 years ago – although, I must say, healthcare, dental care and laws about not killing each other do represent some rather significant progress!

Yet we carry on living with the illusion that the world we inhabit is the simplest and best of all possible worlds. If we go on allowing adverts, messages, news and the media to influence us, we'll almost inevitably end up in a chronic state of despair. The society and the culture we have created is, essentially, an unnatural environment for our organism. This means that it's more essential than ever for you to choose for yourself how you want to be programmed. Do you want to allow others to programme you and lead a life of passive inertia, or would you prefer to determine for yourself who to be, both now and in the future? Do you want to feel better? Do you want to be happier? If you do, my challenge to you is to take charge and create yourself. How you want to programme yourself, which thoughts you choose to think, which people you choose to associate with, which books you choose to read, which news you choose to avoid, and which food you choose to eat. When I freed myself from my depression, I realized that I had allowed myself to become a mere product of all the easy choices society presents us with. I exercised and I ate well, but I was constantly struggling with stress because of the programming that I had received from the social structures that dominate our society. I believed that success meant working a lot, working hard, getting rich and owning lots of stuff. That's absolute bullshit. Success is becoming the best version of yourself! It's choosing actions and thoughts that help you feel good about yourself. When you've attained that state, there's nothing you can't achieve.

There is no quick fix to happiness. Happiness is a lifestyle.

Thanks

This book would never have come about if it weren't for my self-leadership guru and wife Maria Phillips. I also want to thank my incredibly wise children, Anthon, Tristan and Leona, for all the exciting daily conversations we've had, and for all your thoughts on these subjects. Thanks are due to all the thousands of participants who have enrolled in my course in self-leadership and kindly shared feedback with me. Thanks also to David Klemetz for our invaluable collaboration. I would also like to thank my wonderful publisher, Adam Dahlin, for all his words of encouragement along the way, and of course Edith and Maria for helping me as international agents to get this book into your hands. Finally, I want to thank myself for learning to live a life of self-leadership. It's the best decision I've ever made.

The Resource Package

Would you like to continue this path of growth?

The code below will take you to the unique resource package we've prepared for this book, which includes a workbook, inspiring videos, exercises, illustrations and guided meditations!

On the page for the resource package, you'll also find information about the WOW course – a course in self-leadership that will transform your life from the ground up. You can also access this resource package by visiting: davidjpphillips.com/resources.

References

Dopamine References

Francesco Fornai *et al.*, 'Intermittent dopaminergic stimulation causes behavioral sensitization in the addicted brain and parkinsonism', *International Review of Neurobiology*, 88 (2009), 371–98 https://pubmed.ncbi.nlm.nih.gov/19897084/

Gordon G. Gallup, Jr, Rebecca L. Burch, Steven M. Platek, 'Does semen have antidepressant properties?', *Archives of Sexual Behavior*, 31:3 (2002), 289–93 https://pubmed.ncbi.nlm.nih.gov/12049024/

Ignacio González-Burgos and Alfredo Feria-Velasco, 'Serotonin/dopamine interaction in memory formation', *Progress in Brain Research*, 172 (2008), 603–23 https://pubmed.ncbi.nlm.nih.gov/18772052/

David Greene and Mark R. Lepper, 'Effects of extrinsic rewards on children's subsequent intrinsic interest', *Child Development*, 45:4 (1974), 1141–5

Yang Li, Afton L. Hassett and Julia S. Seng, 'Exploring the mutual regulation between oxytocin and cortisol as a marker of resilience', *Archives of Psychiatric Nursing*, 33:2 (2019), 164–73 https://pubmed.ncbi.nlm.nih.gov/30927986/

Andrea L. Meltzer, Anastasia Makhanova and Lindsey L. Hicks, 'Quantifying the sexual afterglow: the lingering benefits of

sex and their implications for pair-bonded relationships',
Psychological Science, 28:5 (2017), 587–98 https://pubmed.
ncbi.nlm.nih.gov/28485699/

Ed O'Brien and Robert W. Smith, 'Unconventional consumption methods and enjoying things consumed: recapturing the "first-time" experience', *Personality and Social Psychology Bulletin*, 45:1 (2019), 67–80 https://pubmed.ncbi.nlm.nih.gov/29911504/

P. Srámek *et al.*, 'Human physiological responses to immersion into water of different temperatures', *European Journal of Applied Physiology*, 81:5 (2000), 436–42 https://pubmed.ncbi.nlm.nih.gov/10751106/

Devin Blair Terhune, Jake G. Sullivan and Jaana M. Simola, 'Time dilates after spontaneous blinking', *Current Biology*, 26:11 (2016), 459–60 https://pubmed.ncbi.nlm.nih.gov/27269720/

Sharmili Edwin Thanarajah *et al.*, 'Food intake recruits orosensory and post-ingestive dopaminergic circuits to affect eating desire in humans', *Cell Metabolism*, 29:3 (2019), 695–706 https://pubmed.ncbi.nlm.nih.gov/30595479/

Oxytocin References

Elissar Andari *et al.*, 'Promoting social behavior with oxytocin in high-functioning autism spectrum disorders', *Proceedings of the National Academy of Sciences*, 107:9 (2010), 4389–94 https://pubmed.ncbi.nlm.nih.gov/20160081/

B. Auyeung *et al.*, 'Oxytocin increases eye contact during a real-time, naturalistic social interaction in males with and without autism', *Translational Psychiatry*, 5:2 (2015) https://pubmed.ncbi.nlm.nih.gov/25668435/

Jorge A. Barraza and Paul J. Zak, 'Empathy toward strangers triggers oxytocin release and subsequent generosity', *Annals of the New York Academy of Sciences*, 1167 (2009), 182–9 https://pubmed.ncbi.nlm.nih.gov/19580564/

Navjot Bhullar, Glenn Surman and Nicola S. Schutte, 'Dispositional gratitude mediates the relationship between a past-positive temporal frame and well-being', *Personality and Individual Differences*, 76 (2015), 52–5 https://www.sciencedirect.com/science/article/abs/pii/S0191886914006576

Guilherme Brockington *et al.*, 'Storytelling increases oxytocin and positive emotions and decreases cortisol and pain in hospitalized children', *Proceedings of the National Academy of Sciences*, 118:22 (2021) https://pubmed.ncbi.nlm.nih.gov/34031240/

Claudia Camerino *et al.*, 'Evaluation of short and long term cold stress challenge of nerve grow factor, brain-derived neurotrophic factor, osteocalcin and oxytocin mRNA expression in BAT, brain, bone and reproductive tissue of male mice using real-time PCR and linear correlation analysis', *Frontiers in Physiology*, 8 (2018), 1101 https://pubmed.ncbi.nlm.nih.gov/29375393/

Tiany W. Chhuom and Hilaire J. Thompson, 'Older spousal dyads and the experience of recovery in the year after traumatic brain injury', *Journal of Neuroscience Nursing*, 53:2 (2021), 57–62 https://pubmed.ncbi.nlm.nih.gov/33538455/

Elizabeth R. Cluett *et al.*, 'Randomised controlled trial of labouring in water compared with standard of augmentation for management of dystocia in first stage of labour', *British*

Medical Journal, 328:7435 (2004), 314 https://pubmed.ncbi.
nlm.nih.gov/14744822/

Sheldon Cohen *et al.*, 'Does hugging provide stress-buffering
social support? A study of susceptibility to upper respira-
tory infection and illness', *Psychological Science*, 26:2 (2015),
135–47 https://pubmed.ncbi.nlm.nih.gov/25526910/

Courtney E. Detillion *et al.*, 'Social facilitation of wound healing', *Psychoneuroendocrinology*, 29:8 (2004), 1004–11 https://
pubmed.ncbi.nlm.nih.gov/15219651/

Burel R. Goodin, Timothy J. Ness and Meredith T. Robbins,
'Oxytocin – a multifunctional analgesic for chronic deep
tissue pain', *Current Pharmaceutical Design*, 21:7 (2015), 906–13
https://pubmed.ncbi.nlm.nih.gov/25345612/

Christina Grape *et al.*, 'Does singing promote well-being?
An empirical study of professional and amateur singers
during a singing lesson', *Integrative Physiological and Behavioral
Science*, 38:1 (2003), 65–74 https://pubmed.ncbi.nlm.nih.
gov/12814197/

Rafael T. Han *et al.*, 'Long-term isolation elicits depression and
anxiety-related behaviors by reducing oxytocin-induced
GABAergic transmission in central amygdala', *Frontiers in
Molecular Neuroscience*, 11 (2018), 246 https://pubmed.ncbi.
nlm.nih.gov/30158853/

Jonne O. Hietanen, Mikko J. Peltola and Jari K. Hietanen, 'Psy-
chophysiological responses to eye contact in a live interaction
and in video call', *Psychophysiology*, 57:6 (2020) https://
pubmed.ncbi.nlm.nih.gov/32320067/

Julianne Holt-Lunstad, Wendy A. Birmingham and Kathleen
C. Light, 'Influence of a "warm touch" support enhance-
ment intervention among married couples on ambulatory

blood pressure, oxytocin, alpha amylase, and cortisol', *Psychosomatic Medicine*, 70:9 (2008), 976–85 https://pubmed.ncbi.nlm.nih.gov/18842740/

René Hurlemann *et al.*, 'Oxytocin enhances amygdala-dependent, socially reinforced learning and emotional empathy in humans', *Journal of Neuroscience*, 30:14 (2010), 4999–5007 https://pubmed.ncbi.nlm.nih.gov/20371820/

Christian Krekel, George Ward and Jan-Emmanuel De Neve, 'Employee wellbeing, productivity, and firm performance', Saïd Business School WP 2019–04 (2019) https://papers.ssrn.com/sol3/papers.cfm?abstract_id=3356581

Jyothika Kumar, Birgit Völlm and Lena Palaniyappan, 'Oxytocin affects the connectivity of the precuneus and the amygdala: a randomized, double-blinded, placebo-controlled neuroimaging trial', *International Journal of Neuropsychopharmacology*, 18:5 (2015) https://pubmed.ncbi.nlm.nih.gov/25522395/

Jyothika Kumar *et al.*, 'Oxytocin modulates the effective connectivity between the precuneus and the dorsolateral prefrontal cortex', *European Archives of Psychiatry and Clinical Neuroscience*, 270:5 (2020), 567–76 https://pubmed.ncbi.nlm.nih.gov/30734090/

G. Lindseth, B. Helland and J. Caspers, 'The effects of dietary tryptophan on affective disorders', *Archives of Psychiatric Nursing*, 29:2 (2015), 102–7 https://pubmed.ncbi.nlm.nih.gov/25858202/

Jinting Liu *et al.*, 'The association between well-being and the COMT gene: dispositional gratitude and forgiveness as mediators', *Journal of Affective Disorders*, 214 (2017), 115–121 https://pubmed.ncbi.nlm.nih.gov/28288405/

R. McCraty *et al.*, 'The impact of a new emotional self-management program on stress, emotions, heart rate variability, DHEA and cortisol', *Integrative Physiological and Behavioral Science*, 33:2 (1998), 151–70 https://pubmed.ncbi.nlm.nih.gov/9737736/

Andrea L. Meltzer *et al.*, 'Quantifying the sexual afterglow: the lingering benefits of sex and their implications for pair-bonded relationships', *Psychological Science*, 28:5 (2017), 587–98 https://pubmed.ncbi.nlm.nih.gov/28485699/

Rachel A. Millstein *et al.*, 'The effects of optimism and gratitude on adherence, functioning and mental health following an acute coronary syndrome', *General Hospital Psychiatry*, 43 (2016), 17–22 https://pubmed.ncbi.nlm.nih.gov/27796252/

Kerstin Uvnäs Moberg and Maria Petersson, '[Oxytocin, a mediator of anti-stress, well-being, social interaction, growth and healing]', *Zeitschrift fur Psychosomatische Medizin und Psychotherapie*, 51:1 (2005), 57–80 https://pubmed.ncbi.nlm.nih.gov/15834840/

Kerstin Uvnäs Moberg, Linda Handlin and Maria Petersson, 'Self-soothing behaviors with particular reference to oxytocin release induced by non-noxious sensory stimulation', *Frontiers in Psychology*, 5 (2015), 1529 https://pubmed.ncbi.nlm.nih.gov/25628581/

Vera Morhenn, Laura E. Beavin and Paul J. Zak, 'Massage increases oxytocin and reduces adrenocorticotropin hormone in humans', *Alternative Therapies in Health and Medicine*, 18:6 (2012), 11–18 https://pubmed.ncbi.nlm.nih.gov/23251939/

Miho Nagasawa *et al.*, 'Oxytocin-gaze positive loop and the coevolution of human–dog bonds', *Science*, 348 (2015), 333–6 https://pubmed.ncbi.nlm.nih.gov/25883356/

Ulrica Nilsson, 'Soothing music can increase oxytocin levels during bed rest after open-heart surgery: a randomised control trial', *Journal of Clinical Nursing*, 17:15 (2009), 2153–61 https://pubmed.ncbi.nlm.nih.gov/19583647/

Miranda Olff *et al.*, 'The role of oxytocin in social bonding, stress regulation and mental health: an update on the moderating effects of context and interindividual differences', *Psychoneuroendocrinology*, 38:9 (2013), 1883–94 https://pubmed.ncbi.nlm.nih.gov/23856187/

Yuuki Ooishi *et al.*, 'Increase in salivary oxytocin and decrease in salivary cortisol after listening to relaxing slow-tempo and exciting fast-tempo music', *PLOS One*, 12:12 (2017) https://pubmed.ncbi.nlm.nih.gov/29211795/

Else Ouweneel, Pascale M. Le Blanc and Wilmar B. Schaufeli, 'On being grateful and kind: results of two randomized controlled trials on study-related emotions and academic engagement', *Journal of Psychology*, 148:1 (2014), 37–60 https://pubmed.ncbi.nlm.nih.gov/24617270/

Narun Pornpattananangkul *et al.*, 'Generous to whom? The influence of oxytocin on social discounting', *Psychoneuroendocrinology*, 79 (2017), 93–7 https://pubmed.ncbi.nlm.nih.gov/28273587/

Michael J. Poulin and E. Alison Holman, 'Helping hands, healthy body? Oxytocin receptor gene and prosocial behavior interact to buffer the association between stress and physical health', *Hormones and Behavior*, 63:3 (2013), 510–17 https://pubmed.ncbi.nlm.nih.gov/23354128/

L. Pruimboom and D. Reheis, 'Intermittent drinking, oxytocin and human health', *Medical Hypotheses*, 92 (2016), 80–83 https://pubmed.ncbi.nlm.nih.gov/27241263/

Feng Sheng *et al.*, 'Oxytocin modulates the racial bias in neural responses to others' suffering', *Biological Psychology*, 92:2 (2013),380–86https://pubmed.ncbi.nlm.nih.gov/23246533/

Jennie R. Stevenson *et al.*, 'Oxytocin administration prevents cellular aging caused by social isolation', *Psychoneuroendocrinology*, 103 (2019), 52–60 https://pubmed.ncbi.nlm.nih.gov/30640038/

Virginia E. Sturm *et al.*, 'Big Smile, Small Self: awe walks promote prosocial positive emotions in older adults', *Emotion*, 22:5 (2022), 1044–58https://pubmed.ncbi.nlm.nih.gov/32955293/

Patty van Cappellen *et al.*, 'Effects of oxytocin administration on spirituality and emotional responses to meditation', *Social Cognitive and Affective Neuroscience*, 11:10 (2016), 1579–87 https://pubmed.ncbi.nlm.nih.gov/27317929/

Michiel van Elk *et al.*, 'The neural correlates of the awe experience: reduced default mode network activity during feelings of awe', *Human Brain Mapping*, 40:12 (2019), 3561–74 https://pubmed.ncbi.nlm.nih.gov/31062899/

Amanda Venta *et al.*, 'Paradoxical effects of intranasal oxytocin on trust in inpatient and community adolescents', *Journal of Clinical Child and Adolescent Psychology*, 48:5 (2019), 706–15 https://pubmed.ncbi.nlm.nih.gov/29236527/

Hasse Walum *et al.*, 'Variation in the oxytocin receptor gene is associated with pair-bonding and social behavior', *Biological Psychiatry*, 71:5 (2012), 419–26 https://pubmed.ncbi.nlm.nih.gov/22015110/

236

Y. Joel Wong *et al.*, 'Does gratitude writing improve the mental health of psychotherapy clients? Evidence from a randomized controlled trial', *Psychotherapy Research*, 28:2 (2018), 192–202 https://pubmed.ncbi.nlm.nih.gov/27139595/

Paul J. Zak *et al.*, 'Oxytocin release increases with age and is associated with life satisfaction and prosocial behaviors', *Frontiers in Behavioral Neuroscience*, 16 (2022) https://pubmed.ncbi.nlm.nih.gov/35530727/

Paul J. Zak, 'Why inspiring stories make us react: the neuroscience of narrative', *Cerebrum* (2 February 2015) https://pubmed.ncbi.nlm.nih.gov/26034526/

Serotonin References

Jon Cooper, 'Stress and Depression', WebMD website (2021) https://www.webmd.com/depression/features/stress-depression

D. H. Edwards and E. A. Kravitz, 'Serotonin, social status and aggression', *Current Opinion in Neurobiology*, 7:6 (1997), 812–19 https://pubmed.ncbi.nlm.nih.gov/9464985/

Amy Fiske, Julie Loebach Wetherell and Margaret Gatz, 'Depression in older adults', *Annual Review of Clinical Psychology*, 5 (2009), 363–89 https://pubmed.ncbi.nlm.nih.gov/19327033/

Lara C. Foland-Ross *et al.*, 'Recalling happier memories in remitted depression: a neuroimaging investigation of the repair of sad mood', *Cognitive, Affective and Behavioral Neuroscience*, 14:2 (2014), 818–826 https://www.ncbi.nlm.nih.gov/pmc/articles/PMC3995858/

Fae Diana Ford, 'Exploring the impact of negative and positive self-talk in relation to loneliness and self-esteem in secondary school-aged adolescents' (dissertation, University of Bolton, 2015) https://e-space.mmu.ac.uk/id/eprint/583488

Knut A. Hestad *et al.*, 'The relationships among tryptophan, kynurenine, indoleamine 2,3-dioxygenase, depression, and neuropsychological performance', *Frontiers in Psychology*, 8 (2017), 1561 https://pubmed.ncbi.nlm.nih.gov/29046648/

Huberman Lab Podcast 34, 'Understanding and Conquering Depression', 2021 https://hubermanlab.com/understanding-and-conquering-depression/

Wayne J. Korzan and Cliff H. Summers, 'Evolution of stress responses refine mechanisms of social rank', *Neurobiology of Stress*, 14 (2021) https://pubmed.ncbi.nlm.nih.gov/33997153/

Brian E. Leonard, 'The concept of depression as a dysfunction of the immune system', *Current Immunology Reviews*, 6:3 (2010), 205–12 https://pubmed.ncbi.nlm.nih.gov/21170282/

Karen-Anne McVey Neufeld *et al.*, 'Oral selective serotonin reuptake inhibitors activate vagus nerve dependent gut–brain signalling', *Scientific Reports*, 9:1 (2019) https://pubmed.ncbi.nlm.nih.gov/31582799/

M. Maes *et al.*, 'The new "5-HT" hypothesis of depression: cell-mediated immune activation induces indoleamine 2,3-dioxygenase, which leads to lower plasma tryptophan and an increased synthesis of detrimental tryptophan catabolites (TRYCATs), both of which contribute to the onset of depression', *Progress in Neuro-Psychopharmacology and Biological Psychiatry*, 35:3 (2011), 702–21 https://pubmed.ncbi.nlm.nih.gov/21185346/

Saruja Nanthakumaran *et al.*, 'The gut–brain axis and its role in depression', *Cureus*, 12:9 (2020) https://pubmed.ncbi.nlm.nih.gov/33042715/

Rhonda P. Patrick and Bruce N. Ames, 'Vitamin D and the omega-3 fatty acids control serotonin synthesis and action, part 2: relevance for ADHD, bipolar disorder, schizophrenia, and impulsive behavior', *FASEB Journal*, 29:6 (2015), 2207–22 https://pubmed.ncbi.nlm.nih.gov/25713056/

A. R. Peirson and J. W. Heuchert, 'Correlations for serotonin levels and measures of mood in a nonclinical sample', *Psychological Reports*, 87:3 Pt 1 (2000), 707–16 https://pubmed.ncbi.nlm.nih.gov/11191371/

Sue Penckofer *et al.*, 'Vitamin D and depression: where is all the sunshine?' *Issues in Mental Health Nursing*, 31:6 (2010), 385–93 https://pubmed.ncbi.nlm.nih.gov/20450340/

M. J. Raleigh *et al.*, 'Serotonergic influences on the social behavior of vervet monkeys (*Cercopithecus aethiops sabaeus*)', *Experimental Neurology*, 68:2 (1980), 322–34 https://pubmed.ncbi.nlm.nih.gov/6444893/

M. J. Raleigh *et al.*, 'Serotonergic mechanisms promote dominance acquisition in adult male vervet monkeys', *Brain Research*, 559:2 (1991), 181–90 https://pubmed.ncbi.nlm.nih.gov/1794096/

Randy A. Sansone and Lori A. Sansone, 'Sunshine, serotonin, and skin: a partial explanation for seasonal patterns in psychopathology?' *Innovations in Clinical Neuroscience*, 10:7–8 (2013), 20–24 https://pubmed.ncbi.nlm.nih.gov/24062970/

Robert Sapolsky, *Why Zebras Don't Get Ulcers* (third edition, Holt, 2004)

B. Spring, 'Recent research on the behavioral effects of trypto-phan and carbohydrate', *Nutrition and Health*, 3:1–2 (1984), 55–67 https://pubmed.ncbi.nlm.nih.gov/6400041/

Martin Stoffel *et al.*, 'Effects of mindfulness-based stress preven-tion on serotonin transporter gene methylation', *Psychotherapy and Psychosomatics*, 88:5 (2019), 317–19 https://pubmed.ncbi.nlm.nih.gov/31461722/

David Tod, James Hardy and Emily Oliver, 'Effects of self-talk: a systematic review', *Journal of Sport and Exercise Psychology*, 33:5 (2011), 666–87 https://pubmed.ncbi.nlm.nih.gov/21984641/

A. E. Tyrer *et al.*, 'Serotonin transporter binding is reduced in seasonal affective disorder following light therapy', *Acta Psychiatrica Scandinavica*, 134:5 (2016), 410–19 https://pubmed.ncbi.nlm.nih.gov/27553523/

Nora D. Volkow *et al.*, 'Evidence that sleep deprivation down-regulates dopamine D_2R in ventral striatum in the human brain', *Journal of Neuroscience*, 32:19 (2012), 6711–17 https://pubmed.ncbi.nlm.nih.gov/22573693/

Nadja Walter, Lucie Nikoleizig and Dorothee Alfermann, 'Effects of self-talk training on competitive anxiety, self-efficacy, volitional skills, and performance: an intervention study with junior sub-elite athletes', *Sports*, 7:6 (2019), 148 https://pubmed.ncbi.nlm.nih.gov/31248129/

Emma Williams *et al.*, 'Associations between whole-blood serotonin and subjective mood in healthy male volunteers', *Biological Psychology*, 71:2 (2006), 171–4 https://pubmed.ncbi.nlm.nih.gov/15927346/

Anna Ziomkiewicz-Wichary, 'Serotonin and Dominance', in *Encyclopedia of Evolutionary Psychological Science* (2016), 1–4 https://www.researchgate.net/publication/310586509_Serotonin_and_Dominance

Cortisol References

Michael A. P. Bloomfield *et al.*, 'The effects of psychosocial stress on dopaminergic function and the acute stress response', *eLife*, 8 (2019) https://pubmed.ncbi.nlm.nih.gov/31711569/

Alison Wood Brooks, 'Get excited: reappraising pre-performance anxiety as excitement', *Journal of Experimental Psychology: General*, 143:3 (2014), 1144–58 https://pubmed.ncbi.nlm.nih.gov/24364682/

Mansoor D. Burhani and Mark M. Rasenick, 'Fish oil and depression: the skinny on fats', *Journal of Integrative Neuroscience*, 16:s1 (2017), S115–S124 https://pubmed.ncbi.nlm.nih.gov/29254106/

Philip C. Calder, 'Omega-3 fatty acids and inflammatory processes', *Nutrients*, 2:3 (2010), 355–74 https://pubmed.ncbi.nlm.nih.gov/22254027/

Philip C. Calder, 'Omega-3 fatty acids and inflammatory processes: from molecules to man', *Biochemical Society Transactions*, 45:5 (2017), 1105–15 https://pubmed.ncbi.nlm.nih.gov/28900017/

Marlena Colasanto, Sheri Madigan and Daphne J. Korczak, 'Depression and inflammation among children and adolescents: a meta-analysis', *Journal of Affective Disorders*, 277 (2020), 940–48 https://pubmed.ncbi.nlm.nih.gov/33065836/

V. Drapeau *et al.*, 'Is visceral obesity a physiological adaptation to stress?', *Panminerva Medica*, 45:3 (2003), 189–95 https://pubmed.ncbi.nlm.nih.gov/14618117/

Barnaby D. Dunn *et al.*, 'The consequences of effortful emotion regulation when processing distressing material: a comparison of suppression and acceptance', *Behaviour Research and Therapy*, 47:9 (2009), 761–73 https://pubmed.ncbi.nlm.nih.gov/19559401/

Benjamin N. Greenwood *et al.*, 'Exercise-induced stress resistance is independent of exercise controllability and the medial prefrontal cortex', *European Journal of Neuroscience*, 37:3 (2013), 469–78 https://pubmed.ncbi.nlm.nih.gov/23121339/

Jeremy P. Jamieson *et al.*, 'Turning the knots in your stomach into bows: reappraising arousal improves performance on the GRE', *Journal of Experimental Social Psychology*, 46:1 (2010), 208–12 https://pubmed.ncbi.nlm.nih.gov/20161454/

Ravinder Jerath *et al.*, 'Self-regulation of breathing as a primary treatment for anxiety', *Applied Psychophysiology and Biofeedback*, 40:2 (2015), 107–15 https://pubmed.ncbi.nlm.nih.gov/25869930/

Chieh-Hsin Lee and Fabrizio Giuliani, 'The role of inflammation in depression and fatigue', *Frontiers in Immunology*, 10 (2019), 1696 https://pubmed.ncbi.nlm.nih.gov/31379879/

Jia-Yi Li *et al.*, 'Voluntary and involuntary running in the rat show different patterns of theta rhythm, physical activity, and heart rate', *Journal of Neurophysiology*, 111:10 (2014), 2061–70 https://pubmed.ncbi.nlm.nih.gov/24623507/

Xiao Ma *et al.*, 'The effect of diaphragmatic breathing on attention, negative affect and stress in healthy adults',

Frontiers in Psychology, 8 (2017), 874 https://pubmed.ncbi.
nlm.nih.gov/28626434/

Robyn J. McQuaid *et al.*, 'Relations between plasma oxytocin
and cortisol: the stress buffering role of social support', *Neurobiology of Stress*, 3 (2016), 52–60 https://pubmed.ncbi.nlm.
nih.gov/27981177/

Emanuele Felice Osimo *et al.*, 'Prevalence of low-grade inflammation in depression: a systematic review and meta-analysis
of CRP levels', *Psychological Medicine*, 49:12 (2019), 1958–70
https://pubmed.ncbi.nlm.nih.gov/31258105/

Jan-Marino Ramirez, 'The integrative role of the sigh in psychology, physiology, pathology, and neurobiology', *Progress
in Brain Research*, 209 (2014), 91–129 https://pubmed.ncbi.
nlm.nih.gov/24746045/

Marc A. Russo, Danielle M. Santarelli and Dean O'Rourke,
'The physiological effects of slow breathing in the healthy
human', *Breathe* (Sheff), 13:4 (2017), 298–309 https://
pubmed.ncbi.nlm.nih.gov/29209423/

Jisun So *et al.*, 'EPA and DHA differentially modulate monocyte
inflammatory response in subjects with chronic inflammation
in part via plasma specialized pro-resolving lipid mediators: a
randomized, double-blind, crossover study', *Atherosclerosis*, 316
(2021), 90–98 https://pubmed.ncbi.nlm.nih.gov/33303222/

Martina Svensson *et al.*, 'Forced treadmill exercise can induce
stress and increase neuronal damage in a mouse model of
global cerebral ischemia', *Neurobiology of Stress*, 5 (2016), 8–18
https://pubmed.ncbi.nlm.nih.gov/27981192/

Zhuxi Yao *et al.*, 'Higher chronic stress is associated with a
decrease in temporal sensitivity but not in subjective

duration in healthy young men', *Frontiers in Psychology*, 6 (2015), 1010 https://pubmed.ncbi.nlm.nih.gov/26257674/

Kaeli W. Yuen *et al.*, 'Plasma oxytocin concentrations are lower in depressed vs. healthy control women and are independent of cortisol', *Journal of Psychiatric Research*, 51 (2014), 30–36 https://pubmed.ncbi.nlm.nih.gov/24405552/

Andrea Zaccaro *et al.*, 'How breath-control can change your life: a systematic review on psycho-physiological correlates of slow breathing', *Frontiers in Human Neuroscience*, 12 (2018), 353 https://pubmed.ncbi.nlm.nih.gov/30245619/

Jing Zhang *et al.*, 'Voluntary wheel running reverses deficits in social behavior induced by chronic social defeat stress in mice: involvement of the dopamine system', *Frontiers in Neuroscience*, 13 (2019), 256 https://pubmed.ncbi.nlm.nih.gov/31019446/

Endorphins References

Ernest L. Abel and Michael L. Kruger, 'Smile intensity in photographs predicts longevity', *Psychological Science*, 21:4 (2010), 542–4 https://pubmed.ncbi.nlm.nih.gov/20424098/

Tobias Becher *et al.*, 'Brown adipose tissue is associated with cardiometabolic health', *Nature Medicine*, 27:1 (2021), 58–65 https://pubmed.ncbi.nlm.nih.gov/33398160/

N. A. Coles, J. T. Larsen and H. C. Lench, 'A meta-analysis of the facial feedback literature: effects of facial feedback on emotional experience are small and variable', *Psychological Bulletin*, 145:6 (2019), 610–51 https://doi.org/10.1037/bul0000194

Dariush Dfarhud, Maryam Malmir and Mohammad Khanah-madi, 'Happiness & health: the biological factors-systematic review article', *Iranian Journal of Public Health*, 43:11 (2014), 1468–77 https://pubmed.ncbi.nlm.nih.gov/26060713/

Barnaby D. Dunn *et al.*, 'The consequences of effortful emotion regulation when processing distressing material: a comparison of suppression and acceptance', *Behaviour Research and Therapy*, 47:9 (2009), 761–73 https://pubmed.ncbi.nlm.nih.gov/19559401/

T. Najafi Ghezeljeh, F. Mohades Ardebili and F. Rafii, 'The effects of massage and music on pain, anxiety and relaxation in burn patients: randomized controlled clinical trial', *Burns*, 43:5 (2017), 1034–43 https://pubmed.ncbi.nlm.nih.gov/28169080/

L. Harker and D. Keltner, 'Expression of positive emotion in women's college yearbook pictures and their relationship to personality and life outcomes across adulthood', *Journal of Personality and Social Psychology*, 80:1 (2001), 112–24 https://pubmed.ncbi.nlm.nih.gov/11195884/

Matthew J. Hertenstein *et al.*, 'Smile intensity in photographs predicts divorce later in life', *Motivation and Emotion*, 33:2 (2009), 99–105 https://link.springer.com/article/10.1007/s11031-009-9124-6

Thea Magrone, Matteo Antonio Russo and Emilio Jirillo, 'Cocoa and dark chocolate polyphenols: from biology to clinical applications', *Frontiers in Immunology*, 8 (2017), 677 https://pubmed.ncbi.nlm.nih.gov/28649251/

Sandra Manninen *et al.*, 'Social laughter triggers endogenous opioid release in humans', *Journal of Neuroscience*, 37:25 (2017), 6152–31 https://pubmed.ncbi.nlm.nih.gov/28536272/

Anthony Papa and George A. Bonnano, 'Smiling in the face of adversity: the interpersonal and intrapersonal functions of smiling', *Emotion*, 8:1 (2008), 1–12 https://pubmed.ncbi.nlm.nih.gov/18266511/

Eiluned Pearce *et al.*, 'Variation in the β-endorphin, oxytocin, and dopamine receptor genes is associated with different dimensions of human sociality', *Proceedings of the National Academy of Sciences*, 114:20 (2017), 5300–305 https://pubmed.ncbi.nlm.nih.gov/28461468/

Lawrence Ian Reed, Rachel Stratton and Jessica D. Rambeas, 'Face value and cheap talk: how smiles can increase or decrease the credibility of our words', *Evolutionary Psychology*, 16:4 (2018) https://pubmed.ncbi.nlm.nih.gov/30497296/

L. Schwarz and W. Kindermann, 'Changes in beta-endorphin levels in response to aerobic and anaerobic exercise', *Sports Medicine*, 13:1 (1992), 25–36 https://pubmed.ncbi.nlm.nih.gov/1553453/

Sophie Scott *et al.*, 'The social life of laughter', *Trends in Cognitive Sciences*, 18:12 (2014), 618–20 https://pubmed.ncbi.nlm.nih.gov/25439499/

Takahiro Seki *et al.*, 'Brown-fat-mediated tumour suppression by cold-altered global metabolism', *Nature*, 608:7922 (2022), 421–8 https://pubmed.ncbi.nlm.nih.gov/35922508/

Nikolai A. Shevchuk, 'Adapted cold shower as a potential treatment for depression', *Medical Hypotheses*, 70:5 (2007), 995–1001 https://pubmed.ncbi.nlm.nih.gov/17993252/

Bronwyn Tarr, Jacques Launay and Robin I. M. Dunbar, 'Silent disco: dancing in synchrony leads to elevated pain thresholds and social closeness', *Evolution and Human Behavior*, 37:5 (2016), 343–9 https://pubmed.ncbi.nlm.nih.gov/27540276/

Bronwyn Tarr *et al.*, 'Synchrony and exertion during dance independently raise pain threshold and encourage social bonding', *Biology Letters*, 11:10 (2015) https://pubmed.ncbi.nlm.nih.gov/26510676/

Testosterone References

Coren L. Apicella, Anna Dreber and Johanna Mollerström, 'Salivary testosterone change following monetary wins and losses predicts future financial risk-taking', *Psychoneuroendocrinology*, 39 (2014), 58–64 https://pubmed.ncbi.nlm.nih.gov/24275004/

Zeki Ari *et al.*, 'Serum testosterone, growth hormone, and insulin-like growth factor-1 levels, mental reaction time, and maximal aerobic exercise in sedentary and long-term physically trained elderly males', *International Journal of Neuroscience*, 114:5 (2004), 623–37 https://pubmed.ncbi.nlm.nih.gov/15204068/

Paul C. Bernhardt *et al.*, 'Testosterone changes during vicarious experiences of winning and losing among fans at sporting events', *Physiology & Behavior*, 65:1 (1998), 59–62

Patricio S. Dalton and Sayantan Ghosal, 'Self-confidence, overconfidence and prenatal testosterone exposure: evidence from the lab', *Frontiers in Behavioral Neuroscience*, 12:5 (2018) https://pubmed.ncbi.nlm.nih.gov/29441000/

T. Babayi Daylari *et al.*, 'Influence of various intensities of 528 Hz sound-wave in production of testosterone in rat's brain and analysis of behavioral changes', *Genes & Genomics*, 41:2 (2019), 201–11 https://pubmed.ncbi.nlm.nih.gov/30414050/

Hirokazu Doi *et al.*, 'Negative correlation between salivary testosterone concentration and preference for sophisticated music in males', *Personality and Individual Differences*, 125 (2018), 106–11 https://www.sciencedirect.com/science/article/abs/pii/S0191886917306980?via%3Dihub

David A. Edwards, Karen Wetzel and Dana R. Wyner, 'Intercollegiate soccer: saliva cortisol and testosterone are elevated during competition, and testosterone is related to status and social connectedness with team mates', *Physiology & Behavior*, 87:1 (2006), 135–43 https://pubmed.ncbi.nlm.nih.gov/16233905/

Kaoutar Ennour-Idrissi, Elizabeth Maunsell and Caroline Diorio, 'Effect of physical activity on sex hormones in women: a systematic review and meta-analysis of randomized controlled trials', *Breast Cancer Research*, 17:1 (2015), 139 https://pubmed.ncbi.nlm.nih.gov/26541144/

Hajime Fukui, 'Music and testosterone: a new hypothesis for the origin and function of music', *Annals of the New York Academy of Sciences*, 930 (2001), 448–51 https://pubmed.ncbi.nlm.nih.gov/11458865/

W. J. Kraemer *et al.*, 'The effects of short-term resistance training on endocrine function in men and women', *European Journal of Applied Physiology and Occupational Physiology*, 78:1 (1998), 69–76 https://pubmed.ncbi.nlm.nih.gov/9660159/

Jennifer Kurath and Rui Mata, 'Individual differences in risk taking and endogeneous [sic] levels of testosterone, estradiol, and cortisol: a systematic literature search and three independent meta-analyses', *Neuroscience & Biobehavioral Reviews*, 90 (2018), 428–46 https://pubmed.ncbi.nlm.nih.gov/29730483/

Hana H. Kutlikova *et al.*, 'Not giving up: testosterone promotes persistence against a stronger opponent', *Psychoneuroendocrinology*, 128 (2021) https://pubmed.ncbi.nlm.nih.gov/33836382/

A. B. Losecaat Vermeer *et al.*, 'Exogenous testosterone increases status-seeking motivation in men with unstable low social status', *Psychoneuroendocrinology*, 113 (2019) https://pubmed.ncbi.nlm.nih.gov/31884320/

Gideon Nave *et al.*, 'Single dose testosterone administration impairs cognitive reflection in men', *Psychological Science*, 28:10 (2017), 1398–1407 https://authors.library.caltech.edu/records/5hvnh-78w12

Marty Nemko, 'From Stress to Genes, Baboons to Hormones', *Psychology Today* website (2017) https://www.psychologytoday.com/gb/blog/how-do-life/201702/stress-genes-baboons-hormones

T. Oliveira, M. J. Gouveia and R. F. Oliveira, 'Testosterine responsiveness to winning and losing experiences in female soccer players', *Psychoneuroendocrinology*, 34:7 (2009), 1056–64 https://pubmed.ncbi.nlm.nih.gov/19278791/

Paola Sapienza, Luigi Zingales and Dario Maestripieri, 'Gender differences in financial risk aversion and career choices are affected by testosterone', *Proceedings of the National Academy of Sciences*, 106:36 (2009), 15268–73 https://pubmed.ncbi.nlm.nih.gov/19706398/

Oliver C. Schultheiss, Michelle M. Wirth and Steven J. Stanton, 'Effects of affiliation and power motivation on salivary progesterone and testosterone', *Hormones and Behavior*, 46:5 (2004), 592–9 https://pubmed.ncbi.nlm.nih.gov/15555501/

Maureen M. J. Smeets-Janssen *et al.*, 'Salivary testosterone is consistently and positively associated with extraversion:

results from the Netherlands Study of Depression and Anxiety', *Neuropsychobiology*, 71:2 (2015), 76–84 https://pubmed.ncbi.nlm.nih.gov/25871320/

Rafael Timón Andrada *et al.*, 'Variations in urine excretion of steroid hormones after an acute session and after a 4-week programme of strength training', *European Journal of Applied Physiology*, 99:1 (2007), 65–71 https://pubmed.ncbi.nlm.nih.gov/17051372/

Benjamin C. Trumble *et al.*, 'Age-independent increases in male salivary testosterone during horticultural activity among Tsimane forager-farmers', *Evolution and Human Behavior*, 34:5 (2013), 350–57

Diana Vaamonde *et al.*, 'Physically active men show better semen parameters and hormone values than sedentary men', *European Journal of Applied Physiology*, 112:9 (2012), 3267–73 https://pubmed.ncbi.nlm.nih.gov/22234399/

Sari M. van Anders, Jeffrey Steiger and Katherine L. Goldey, 'Effects of gendered behavior on testosterone in women and men', *Proceedings of the National Academy of Sciences*, 112:45 (2015), 13805–10 https://pubmed.ncbi.nlm.nih.gov/26504229/

Yin Wu *et al.*, 'The role of social status and testosterone in human conspicuous consumption', *Scientific Reports*, 7:1 (2017) https://pubmed.ncbi.nlm.nih.gov/28924142/

Meditation References

Julia C. Basso *et al.*, 'Brief, daily meditation enhances attention, memory, mood, and emotional regulation in non-experienced meditators', *Behavioural Brain Research*, 356 (2019), 208–220 https://pubmed.ncbi.nlm.nih.gov/30153464/

Manoj K. Bhasin *et al.*, 'Specific transcriptome changes associated with blood pressure reduction in hypertensive patients after relaxation response training', *Journal of Alternative and Complementary Medicine*, 24:5 (2018), 486–504 https://pubmed.ncbi.nlm.nih.gov/29616846/

Viviana Capurso, Franco Fabbro and Cristiano Crescentini, 'Mindful creativity: the influence of mindfulness meditation on creative thinking', *Frontiers in Psychology*, 4 (2014) https://pubmed.ncbi.nlm.nih.gov/24454303/

Barbara L. Fredrickson *et al.*, 'Positive emotion correlates of meditation practice: a comparison of mindfulness meditation and loving-kindness meditation', *Mindfulness*, 8:6 (2017) 1623–33 https://pubmed.ncbi.nlm.nih.gov/29201247/

Julieta Galante *et al.*, 'Effect of kindness-based meditation on health and well-being: a systematic review and meta-analysis', *Journal of Consulting and Clinical Psychology*, 82:6 (2014), 1101–14 https://pubmed.ncbi.nlm.nih.gov/24979314/

Tim Gard, Britta K. Hölzel and Sara W. Lazar, 'The potential effects of meditation on age-related cognitive decline: a systematic review', *Annals of the New York Academy of Sciences*, 1307 (2014), 89–103 https://pubmed.ncbi.nlm.nih.gov/24571182/

Madhav Goyal *et al.*, 'Meditation programs for psychological stress and well-being: a systematic review and meta-analysis', *JAMA Internal Medicine*, 174:3 (2014), 357–68 https://pubmed.ncbi.nlm.nih.gov/24395196/

Xiaoli He *et al.*, 'The interventional effects of loving-kindness meditation on positive emotions and interpersonal interactions', *Neuropsychiatric Disease and Treatment*, 11 (2015), 1273–7 https://pubmed.ncbi.nlm.nih.gov/26060402/

Stefan G. Hofmann and Angelina F. Gómez, 'Mindfulness-based interventions for anxiety and depression', *Psychiatric Clinics of North America*, 40:4 (2017), 739–49 https://pubmed.ncbi.nlm.nih.gov/29080597/

Felipe A. Jain *et al.*, 'Critical analysis of the efficacy of meditation therapies for acute and subacute phase treatment of depressive disorders: a systematic review', *Psychosomatics*, 56:2 (2015), 140–52 https://pubmed.ncbi.nlm.nih.gov/25591492/

Laura G. Kiken and Natalie J. Shook, 'Does mindfulness attenuate thoughts emphasizing negativity, but not positivity?', *Journal of Research in Personality*, 53 (2014), 22–30 https://pubmed.ncbi.nlm.nih.gov/25284906/

Emily K. Lindsay *et al.*, 'Mindfulness training reduces loneliness and increases social contact in a randomized controlled trial', *Proceedings of the National Academy of Sciences*, 116:9 (2019), 3488–93 https://pubmed.ncbi.nlm.nih.gov/30808743/

Catherine J. Norris *et al.*, 'Brief mindfulness meditation improves attention in novices: evidence from ERPs and moderation by neuroticism', *Frontiers in Human Neuroscience*, 12 (2018), 315 https://pubmed.ncbi.nlm.nih.gov/30127731/

David W. Orme-Johnson and Vernon A. Barnes, 'Effects of the transcendental meditation technique on trait anxiety: a meta-analysis of randomized controlled trials', *Journal of Alternative and Complementary Medicine*, 20:5 (2014), 330–41 https://pubmed.ncbi.nlm.nih.gov/24107199/

Kim Rod, 'Observing the effects of mindfulness-based meditation on anxiety and depression in chronic pain patients',

Psychiatria Danubina, 27:1 (2015), 209–11 https://pubmed. ncbi.nlm.nih.gov/26417764/

Amit Sood and David T. Jones, 'On mind wandering, attention, brain networks, and meditation', *Explore*, 9:3 (2013), 136–41 https://pubmed.ncbi.nlm.nih.gov/23643368/

Yingge Tong *et al.*, 'Effects of tai chi on self-efficacy: a systematic review', *Evidence-Based Complementary and Alternative Medicine* (2018) https://pubmed.ncbi.nlm.nih.gov/30186352/

Miscellaneous References

Rinske A. Gotink *et al.*, '8-week Mindfulness Based Stress Reduction induces brain changes similar to traditional long-term meditation practice: a systematic review', *Brain and Cognition*, 108 (2016), 32–41 https://pubmed.ncbi.nlm.nih. gov/27429096/

Niklas Joisten *et al.*, 'Exercise and the kynurenine pathway: current state of knowledge and results from a randomized cross-over study comparing acute effects of endurance and resistance training', *Exercise Immunology Review*, 26 (2020), 24–42 https://pubmed.ncbi.nlm.nih.gov/32139353/

Kyle S. Martin, Michele Azzolini and Jorge Lira Ruas, 'The kynurenine connection: how exercise shifts muscle tryptophan metabolism and affects energy homeostasis, the immune system, and the brain', *American Journal of Physiology–Cell Physiology*, 318:5 (2020), 818–30 https://pubmed.ncbi. nlm.nih.gov/32208989/

Bernadette Mazurek Melnyk *et al.*, 'Interventions to improve mental health, well-being, physical health, and lifestyle behaviors in physicians and nurses: a systematic review', *American Journal of Health Promotion*, 34:8 (2020), 929–41 https://pubmed.ncbi.nlm.nih.gov/32338522/

Jodi A. Mindell *et al.*, 'A nightly bedtime routine: impact on sleep in young children and maternal mood', *Sleep*, 32:5 (2009), 599–606 https://pubmed.ncbi.nlm.nih.gov/19480226/

Joyce Shaffer, 'Neuroplasticity and clinical practice: building brain power for health', *Frontiers in Psychology*, 7 (2016) https://pubmed.ncbi.nlm.nih.gov/27507957/

H. Vainio, E. Heseltine and J. Wilbourn, 'Priorities for future IARC monographs on the evaluation of carcinogenic risks to humans', *Environmental Health Perspectives*, 102:6–7 (1994), 590–91 https://pubmed.ncbi.nlm.nih.gov/9679121/

Patrice Voss *et al.*, 'Dynamic brains and the changing rules of neuroplasticity: implications for learning and recovery', *Frontiers in Psychology*, 8 (2017) https://pubmed.ncbi.nlm.nih. gov/29085312/